CONTEMPORARY PERSPECTIVES *on* LITERACY

Mastering
MEDIA
LITERACY

Heidi Hayes Jacobs
SERIES EDITOR

Frank W. BAKER

Verneda EDWARDS

Heidi Hayes JACOBS

Jennie L. JOHNSON

Holen Sabrina KAHN

Emily KEATING

Kristy SAILORS

Mark SCHULTE

Solution Tree | Press

a division of

Solution Tree

555 North Morton Street
Bloomington, IN 47404
800.733.6786 (toll free) / 812.336.7700
FAX: 812.336.7790
email: info@solution-tree.com
solution-tree.com

Visit **go.solution-tree.com/21stcenturyskills** to find direct links to the many tools and resources cited in this book.

Printed in the United States of America

17 16 15 14 13   1 2 3 4 5

Library of Congress Cataloging-in-Publication Data

Baker, Frank W. (Educational consultant)

  Mastering media literacy / Frank W. Baker, Verneda Edwards, Heidi Hayes Jacobs, Jennie L. Johnson, Holen Sabrina Kahn, Emily Keating, Kristy Sailors, Mark Schulte.
       pages cm
  Includes bibliographical references and index.
   ISBN 978-1-936764-56-3 (perfect bound) 1. Mass media in education--United States. 2. Media literacy--United States. 3. Media literacy--Study and teaching. I. Title.
   LB1043.B314 2014
   371.33'50973--dc23
                                      2013038678

Solution Tree
Jeffrey C. Jones, CEO
Edmund M. Ackerman, President

Solution Tree Press
President: Douglas M. Rife
Editorial Director: Lesley Bolton
Managing Production Editor: Caroline Weiss
Senior Production Editor: Suzanne Kraszewski
Proofreader: Sarah Payne-Mills
Cover Designer: Jenn Taylor
Text Designer: Laura Kagemann

In Memory

The *Contemporary Perspectives on Literacy* series is dedicated to Jane Bullowa, former assistant superintendent for instructional services at the Ulster Board of Cooperative Educational Services in upstate New York, where she worked for thirty-seven years. It has been my experience that regional service center leaders are among the most talented and forward-thinking educators in the United States. In that tradition, Jane was relentlessly progressive yet had the easiest style. She encouraged innovation and provided educators with opportunities to try out new approaches. In particular, she prompted me to engage in the integration of emerging technologies from the onset of the first CD-ROMs to Netscape Navigator as a browser. I vividly remember the day she introduced me to my first videoconference on a Polycom, and I could see the world expanding in our classrooms. Jane opened learning portals for thousands of students, teachers, and administrators. Thank you, Jane.

—Heidi Hayes Jacobs

Acknowledgments

The process of writing a book is both personal and collaborative. Many individuals contributed to this series, bit by bit, page by page, experience by experience. I want to start with a deeply felt thank you to our chapter authors. Each one of them juggles multiple responsibilities, and I value and appreciate the time and effort each has invested in reflecting on, wrestling with, and defining the new literacies.

In two memorable conversations—one in Melbourne, Australia, and one in San Francisco, California—Douglas Rife, president of Solution Tree Press, prompted me to consider creating the four-book series *Contemporary Perspectives on Literacy*. I am grateful for the personal encouragement and coaching he has provided while concurrently displaying remarkable patience. Outside reviewers, under the direction of Solution Tree Press, gave us solid and incisive feedback on our first drafts that helped our authors rework and craft their text. The editorial staff at Solution Tree Press is of the highest quality, and we continue to appreciate their direction.

Countless numbers of teachers and administrators from around the world work diligently to bring the best to their students every day, and they have provided inspiration for our work at the Curriculum 21 Project. The Curriculum 21 faculty— a group of exceptional professionals—has been supporting educators since the early 2000s. They are an inspiration and a testament to the power of collaboration.

In particular, I want to give a round of applause to Elisa Black and Kathy Scoli for their outstanding and meticulous editorial work preparing chapters for review. Justin Fleisher and Michele Griffin were extremely helpful in assisting me with the research for chapter 4, "Designing a Film Study Curriculum and Canon." Earl Nicholas proved to be a constant anchor and creative soundboard in projects related to merging curriculum and technology.

With constant support and humor, my husband, Jeffrey, is always there for me when I take the plunge into a new project. As always, our adult children, Rebecca and Matt, are my ultimate inspiration.

—Heidi Hayes Jacobs, Series Editor

Solution Tree Press would like to thank the following reviewers:

Allison Butler
Lecturer, Department of Communication
University of Massachusetts Amherst
Amherst, Massachusetts

Jennifer Fleming
Associate Professor, Department of Journalism and Mass Communication
California State University Long Beach
Long Beach, California

Daniel T. Hickey
Associate Professor and Director of Learning Sciences
Counseling and Educational Psychology Department
Indiana University
Bloomington, Indiana

Jeff Share
Teacher Education Program Faculty Advisor
Department of Teacher Education
University of California Los Angeles
Los Angeles, California

Richard Wood
Founder and Consultant
Wood Educational Services, LLC
Warren, Michigan

Visit **go.solution-tree.com/21stcenturyskills** to find direct links to the many tools and resources cited in this book.

Table of Contents

Chapter 5. Examining New Media Journalism: Global Perspectives and Possibilities

By Mark Schulte and Jennie L. Johnson

Index

About the Series Editor

Heidi Hayes Jacobs, EdD, is an internationally recognized expert in the fields of curriculum and instruction. She writes and consults on issues and practices pertaining to curriculum mapping, dynamic instruction, and 21st century strategic planning. She is president of Curriculum Designers and director of the Curriculum 21 Project, whose faculty provides professional development services and support to schools and education organizations. Featured prominently as a speaker at conferences, at workshops, and on webinars, Heidi is noted for her engaging, provocative, and forward-thinking presentations. She is an accomplished author, having published eleven books, journal articles, online media, and software platforms. Above all, Heidi views her profession as grounded in a K–12 perspective thanks to her early years as a high school, middle school, and elementary teacher in Utah, Massachusetts, Connecticut, and New York.

Heidi completed her doctoral work at Columbia University's Teachers College, where she studied under a national Graduate Leadership Fellowship from the U.S. Department of Education. Her master's degree is from the University of Massachusetts Amherst, and she did her undergraduate studies at the University of Utah. She is married, has two adult children, and lives in Rye, New York.

To learn more about Heidi's work, visit www.curriculum21.com and follow her on Twitter @curriculum21 and @heidihayesjacob. To book Heidi for professional development, contact pd@solution-tree.com.

Introduction

By Heidi Hayes Jacobs

To many of us, the label *21st century* conjures up visions of futuristic scenes from Isaac Asimov's writings. Indeed, labeling global, media, and digital literacies as *21st century skills* is a misnomer. In reality, these are *right now* proficiencies—*new literacies*. Even though the future has caught up with us, and the 21st century is right now, we continue to serve students in school systems that operate on a 19th century timetable and deliver a 20th century curriculum. To reference another futuristic author, our education system functions like a Jules Verne time machine, forcing our students to be time travelers between the present and the past.

Nostalgia for the good old days is pervasive in pockets of society, but it is hard to make a convincing case for going backward in the field of education. In my work with U.S. and international schools, I rarely encounter questions about whether or not we should modernize our education system; the pertinent questions are about *how* we should modernize our education system. Grappling with these questions invariably leads to discussion of three new literacies that exponentially empower us to communicate and create with immediacy: global literacy, media literacy, and digital literacy. The *Contemporary Perspectives on Literacy* four-book series is a place to cultivate the discussion of these new literacies.

There are five primary purposes of the series:

1. To clarify each new literacy in order to provide a basis for curriculum and instructional decision making

2. To find the relationship between traditional print and visual literacy and the three new literacies

3. To provide steps and resources to support the cultivation of each literacy in classrooms and virtual learning environments

4. To identify steps and examples of how to lead the transition from older paradigms to the integration of the three literacies in professional development

5. To inform decision makers on the far-reaching effects of policy and organizational structures on the effective modernization of learning environments

A range of perspectives is essential when examining each literacy and how it interacts with others. To that end, the series includes a cohort of writers from a variety of organizations and disciplines—a classroom teacher, a public school district information technology director, a leadership team from an international school, researchers, university professors, the director of a not-for-profit organization devoted to journalism, the founder of an education network, a media critic, a regional service center professional developer, consultants, the leader of a film- and media-making center, and the director of an international society supporting global learning. This team of authors has come together to share views and experiences with the central goal of expanding and contributing to the practice of educators. The commitment of each author to this work is commendable, and I am grateful for their patience and productivity. Working with them has been a remarkable journey.

In this book series, we consider the distinctive characteristics of each new literacy and how schools can integrate them. The new literacies provide exciting possibilities for classrooms, schools, organizations, and social networks. In this book, *Mastering Media Literacy*, we examine how the media mediates our experiences. In our view, media literacy is both generative and responsive; it is the ability to create expression through a wide array of modern media and to critically examine the influx of media from multiple sources. In this book, we turn to specialists with background in media production, journalism, and the classroom.

In chapter 1, "Infusing Media Literacy and Critical Media Analysis Into the Classroom," Frank W. Baker lays a foundation for the discussion. He walks us through the grammar of different media formats and the technical information our learners need to critique media messages—from advertisements to television to film.

Based on their work at the largest education media literacy center in the world, the Jacob Burns Film Center, Emily Keating and Holen Sabrina Kahn give us a structure for creating teaching and learning in chapter 2, "Building a Framework for Literacy in a Visual Culture." Their contribution to media literacy is a thoughtful, well-researched scope and sequence of approaches that will give a backbone to curriculum planning.

In an exciting and new contribution to the field, Verneda Edwards and Kristy Sailors examine the question, How do we assess the quality of student work? In chapter 3, "Creating New Media Rubrics: Quality Student Products for the 21st Century," they draw on several years of fieldwork to examine examples of media and digital tool rubrics and strategies for employing them successfully with students.

When considering media literacy, my colleague Frank W. Baker and I have been frequently perplexed by the dearth of film literature programs in the curriculum. In chapter 4, "Designing a Film Study Curriculum and Canon," we lay out a series of instructional steps a teacher can follow to engage students in a deeper analysis of film study. We also make a case for the cultivation of a film canon in our schools and suggest some possible titles for that canon.

The final chapter brings a fresh angle on media journalism with a global focus. In chapter 5, "Examining New Media Journalism: Global Perspectives and Possibilities," Mark Schulte and Jennie L. Johnson describe the extensive work and contributions of the Pulitzer Center on Crisis Reporting, which provides a wealth of resources for classroom teachers and access to daily reports for students from around the world. This chapter gives educators a fresh angle on how to consider media reporting and can be used to encourage young people to consider careers in the field.

We hope these five chapters will bring different perspectives to the dialogue regarding how to support the shift to new types of learning environments that can integrate digital, media, and global literacy into organizations, teaching practice, administrative styles, and ultimately, into the lives of learners.

We encourage you to connect *Mastering Media Literacy* with the other three companion books in the series for a more complete and detailed examination of the new literacies.

Visit **go.solution-tree.com/21stcenturyskills** to find direct links to the many tools and resources cited in this book.

Frank W. Baker is a much sought-after media literacy education consultant. He has written teaching standards and supporting documents for the state of South Carolina. He is the author of three books; his most recent is *Media Literacy in the K–12 Classroom*. He created and maintains the internationally recognized Media Literacy Clearinghouse website (www .frankwbaker.com/default1.htm), and he conducts media literacy workshops at conferences, schools, and districts across the United States. He is a former consultant to the National Council of Teachers of English and the South Carolina Writing Improvement Network.

To learn more about Frank's work, visit him on Twitter @fbaker or on his blog at www.ncte-ama.blogspot.com.

To book Frank for professional development, contact pd@solution-tree.com.

Chapter 1

Infusing Media Literacy and Critical Media Analysis Into the Classroom

By Frank W. Baker

Surveys of young people's media habits reveal that youth spend more time in front of screens than ever before (Guernsey, 2011). Health experts, including the American Academy of Pediatrics, are already concerned about the impact of this excessive screen time, and some experts worry that today's youth are not reading as much as they used to (Mehegan, 2007). In reality, what they read and how they read has been changed by both media and technology. Today, the screen they pay the most attention to is mobile; they carry it with them at all times, using it to play music and video games, watch movies and television, text, surf the web, upload and download materials, check and update their social media, and of course, talk. The amount and speed of information delivery is dizzying, yet screen media education is slow to become part of the American education system—despite the fact that the screen is a ubiquitous part of our modern-day culture.

As a media literacy educator, I maintain that while our students may be media savvy, most are not media literate. They tend to believe everything they see, read, and hear; they do not possess healthy skepticism. Their K–12 instruction has not provided them with the necessary critical-thinking tools to see through spin, recognize biased reporting, or understand infographics, the visual representation of information and numbers. Indeed, media illiteracy is rampant.

Our students need help to become media literate—to learn the critical-thinking skills necessary to be effective and competent citizens and communicators in the 21st century. In *The Wizard of Oz*, Dorothy is told to "pay no attention to that man behind the curtain." My goal as a media literacy educator is to "pull back the curtain" on how the media work, because, for the most part, students never get the opportunity to see media in production; they see the final product only—not the process or the people behind the scenes. The curtain needs to be pulled way back. As media critic Jean Kilbourne (1999), a longtime advocate for media literacy education, points out:

> Huge and powerful industries—alcohol, tobacco, junk food, guns, diet—depend upon a media-illiterate population. Indeed they depend upon a population that is disempowered and addicted. These industries will and do fight our efforts with all their mighty resources. And we will fight back, using the tools of media education which enable us to understand, analyze, interpret, to expose hidden agendas and manipulation, to bring about constructive change, and to further positive aspects of the media. (p. 305)

Since 1970, when the National Council of Teachers of English (NCTE) first passed a resolution on media literacy, the organization has consistently recommended that teachers include nonprint texts in classrooms, but the Common Core State Standards for English language arts (CCSS ELA), adopted by forty-five states and the District of Columbia at the time of this printing, have virtually ignored media, visual literacy, and media education (Beach & Baker, 2011). A 1999 survey of state standards (Kubey & Baker, 1999) found elements of media literacy in most states' standards for English language arts, but much of that has been wiped out by the adoption of the Common Core ELA standards.

Besides the danger in media illiteracy, there is value in incorporating media into instruction. The Partnership for 21st Century Skills (P21) recognizes media literacy as one of the 21st century skills all students need. It defines media literacy in two ways: analyzing media and creating media.

When students analyze media, they:

- Understand both how and why media messages are constructed, and for what purposes
- Examine how individuals interpret messages differently, how values and points of view are included or excluded, and how media can influence beliefs and behaviors
- Apply a fundamental understanding of the ethical and legal issues surrounding the access and use of media

(P21, n.d.)

When students create media, they:

- Understand and utilize the most appropriate media creation tools, characteristics, and conventions
- Understand and effectively utilize the most appropriate expressions and interpretations in diverse, multicultural environments

(P21, n.d.)

When teachers are properly trained and feel comfortable teaching media literacy, they have a set of important tools for their teaching repertoire. They begin to recognize and appreciate young people's media and their fascination with it. Media literacy encourages teachers to embrace the popular culture of their students, and it provides a hook to get students' interest, which leads to meeting standards and academic achievement.

Text is more than just words on a page, and *literacy* means more than understanding the written word; media are also texts designed to be read, analyzed, interpreted, deconstructed, and created. Media literacy education encourages deep-reading analysis and deconstruction, a process not solely devoted to the printed word. Media literacy's chief objective is critical inquiry: questioning. The approach to teaching media literacy I advocate incorporates elements of visual literacy, concepts like *representation*, an understanding of advertising, and the engaging processes of digital storytelling and filmmaking. I think it's critical that today's educators consider using images and video from both popular culture, the news, and young people's media as the hooks to engage students in learning while at the same time meeting those all-important teaching standards.

Engaging Students in Media Making

When we provide students with cameras—both still and video—we give them innumerable opportunities to be creators, producers, and broadcasters. While some teachers feel video is the enemy of literacy, many others are embracing media production as a meaningful way to teach essential skills, such as writing and persuasion. Some studies on the effects of teaching video production show positive benefits for both students at risk and for gifted students in elementary and secondary grades (Edwards, 2002). Creating digital stories gives students "an opportunity to experiment with self-representation—telling a story that highlights specific characteristics or events—a key part of establishing their identity" (EDUCAUSE Learning Initiative, 2007).

In 2008, Andrew Churches revised Bloom's Taxonomy, relabeling it as Bloom's *Digital* Taxonomy with the verb "creating" now atop the list of higher-order thinking skills. The revised taxonomy suggests schools should be engaging students in the new literacies by having them make media—creating and publishing blogs, films, animation, podcasts, and more. The key terms and verbs in Bloom's Digital Taxonomy (Churches, 2008) are as follows. Churches's additions to Bloom's version appear in italics.

- **Creating**
  - Designing, constructing, planning, producing, inventing, devising, making, *programming, filming, animating, blogging, video blogging, mixing, remixing, wiki-ing, publishing, videocasting, podcasting, directing, producing*

- **Evaluating**
  - Checking, hypothesizing, critiquing, experimenting, judging, testing, detecting, monitoring, *blog or vlog commenting, reviewing, posting, moderating, collaborating, networking, refactoring, alpha and beta testing*

- **Analyzing**
  - Comparing, organizing, deconstructing, attributing, outlining, finding, structuring, integrating, *mashing, linking, tagging, validating reverse-engineering, cracking*

- **Applying**
  - Implementing, carrying out, using, executing, *running, loading, playing, operating, hacking, uploading, sharing, editing*

- **Understanding**
  - Interpreting, summarizing, inferring, paraphrasing, classifying, comparing, explaining, exemplifying, *conducting advanced searches and Boolean searches, blog journaling, twittering, categorizing, commenting, annotating, subscribing*

- **Remembering**
  - Recognizing, listing, describing, identifying, retrieving, naming, locating, finding, *bullet pointing, highlighting, bookmarking, social networking, social bookmarking, "favoriting" and local bookmarking, searching, googling*

Creating involves writing and analyzing. Elizabeth Daley (2003), dean of the University of Southern California School of Cinematic Arts, says students "need to be taught to write for the screen and analyze multimedia just as much as, if not more than, they need to be taught to write and analyze any specific genre in text" (p. 37). Likewise, George Lucas, filmmaker and founder of Edutopia, would like to see 21st century education embrace the teaching of the grammars of the visual and film industries. In a 2004 interview, Lucas urges schools to rethink how English is taught—to embrace communication to include instruction in visual and film literacy, both powerful and persuasive languages in the 21st century (Daly, 2004). Fortunately, free and low-cost software and apps make media production more accessible and easier than ever. Most computers and tablets are equipped with media-making software that make producing video so user-friendly that even a fourth grader can do it. In fact, that's exactly what happened in one school in New York.

In 2008, Class 4-302 at New York City's PS 124 produced a public service announcement (PSA) on the effects of global warming and what can be done about them. The students' four-minute PSA is impressive enough, but in the final production, which can be seen at http://themediaspot.org/videos/ps-124-psa-global-warming-you, they first explain the various production steps they took before they could begin filming. They describe their research, writing the script, creating the storyboards, and production. They also learned about issues of permissions and copyright, as evidenced in the closing credits.

Engaging students in production activities is just one of the goals of media literacy education, the other goal being analysis. When we give students opportunities to analyze media messages, we help them understand how media producers use various techniques to create persuasive and influential communications, for example, both of which are important and relevant skills in the 21st century. If students are going to produce their own PSA, the teacher might take time to show them examples from the Ad Council's website (www.adcouncil.org), such as radio and television announcements and scripts. Analyzing the words, images, and sounds from existing PSAs is a nature first step before students begin to think about producing their own.

Using Media Literacy to Promote Critical Inquiry

Think for a moment about all the ways you experience media. Now, think about how your students experience it. There are many opportunities to bring media texts into instruction. The types of media texts that teachers should consider include, but are not limited to, newspapers and magazines (both in print and in e-formats), television and video, radio, music, advertising (in all of its forms), film, and the Internet. These texts provide ample opportunity for critical inquiry.

The Center for Media Literacy (www.medialit.org) outlines an approach for bringing critical inquiry into the classroom within a framework of media literacy

(Center for Media Literacy, 2011). The center identifies five core media literacy concepts and provides corresponding critical-inquiry questions, as shown in figure 1.1.

CML's Questions/TIPS (Q/TIPS) © **2002–2007 Center for Media Literacy, www.medialit.org**				
Number	**Key Words**	**Deconstruction: CML's Five Key Questions (Consumer)**	**CML's Five Core Concepts**	**Construction: CML's Five Key Questions (Producer)**
1	Authorship	Who created this message?	All media messages are constructed.	What am I authoring?
2	Format	What creative techniques are used to attract my attention?	Media messages are constructed using a creative language with its own rules.	Does my message reflect understanding in format, creativity, and technology?
3	Audience	How might different people understand this message differently?	Different people experience the same media message differently.	Is my message engaging and compelling for my target audience?
4	Content	What values, lifestyles, and points of view are represented in or omitted from this message?	Media have embedded values and points of view.	Have I clearly and consistently framed values, lifestyles, and points of view in my content?
5	Purpose	Why is this message being sent?	Most media messages are organized to gain profit, power, or both.	Have I communicated my purpose effectively?

Figure 1.1: CML's five core concepts and key questions for consumers and producers media deconstruction and construction framework.
Source: Center for Media Literacy, n.d.; CML Questions/TIPS used with permission, Center for Media Literacy, Los Angeles, California, www.medialit.org.

The National Association for Media Literacy Education (NAMLE) takes questioning even further. It created a handout (figure 1.2) with a longer list of questions that teachers are encouraged to print and use in their media education to promote critical inquiry (National Association for Media Literacy Education, 2009).

Audience and authorship	Authorship	Who made this message?
	Purpose	Why was this made? Who is the target audience, and how do you know?
	Economics	Who paid for this?
	Impact	Who might benefit from this message? Who might be harmed by it? Why might this message matter to you?
	Response	What kinds of actions might you take in response to this message?
Messages and meanings	Content	What is this about, and what makes you think that? What ideas, values, information, or points of view are overt? Implied? What is left out of this message that might be important to know?
	Techniques	What techniques are used? Why were those techniques used? How do they communicate the message?
	Interpretations	How might different people understand this message differently? What is your interpretation of this, and what do you learn about yourself from your reaction or interpretation?
Representations and reality	Context	When was this made? Where or how was it shared with the public?
	Credibility	Is this fact, opinion, or something else? How credible is this, and what makes you think that? What are the sources of the information, ideas, or assertions?

Figure 1.2: NAMLE's key questions to ask when analyzing media messages.
Source: Reprinted with permission from NAMLE, 2009. (Formerly AMLA [www.NAMLE.net])

Acknowledging that many teachers are not comfortable teaching popular culture, educator Ryan Goble created the Making Curriculum Pop Ning (http://mcpopmb.ning.com; see figure 1.3). The site is composed of various groups that members can join depending on their interests, subject, or the popular-culture genre they teach. A *Ning* is a resource-sharing site that educators join (for free) in order to connect with other educators about topics of mutual interest. Educators can post items of interest, ask questions of the entire Ning community, or connect with other educators on a topic of interest. One of the most active groups on Making Curriculum Pop is the graphic novels and comics group. Graphic novels have become one of the most popular ways to encourage students not only in reading but also in learning to appreciate both visual literacy and filmmaking, since graphic novels resemble the storyboards created in the filmmaking process. School librarians consistently tell me that the graphic novels they have in their media center collections are often the texts most read by young readers. Students report liking the visual nature of the stories—being able to see the images while reading the text. This new literacy is one that many schools are exploring by not only having students read graphic novels but also by engaging them in creating their own. The graphic novel production process requires them to think about how to visualize the message so that the reader understands the action and narrative.

Figure 1.3: The Making Curriculum Pop Ning social networking website.
Source: Reprinted with permission from Ryan Goble (http://mcpopmb.ning.com).

Turning Students Into Filmmakers

The new literacy movement acknowledges that film is part of the various literacies students should know and appreciate. The Common Core English language arts standards even acknowledge the importance of teaching with and about film, such as in the following examples from grades 7 and 8:

> Compare and contrast a written story, drama, or poem to its audio, filmed, staged, or multimedia version, analyzing the effects of techniques unique to each medium (e.g., lighting, sound, color, or camera focus and angles in a film). (RL.7.7) (NGA & CCSSO, 2010, p. 37)

> Analyze the extent to which a filmed or live production of a story or drama stays faithful to or departs from the text or script, evaluating the choices made by the director or actors. (RL.8.7) (NGA & CCSSO, 2010, p. 37)

We know students love the movies; many learners enjoy retelling the plot, discussing characters, special effects, and more. Since they've already started down the road to film education, it's not difficult for teachers to take them a bit further. Jim Burke (2012), author of *The English Teacher's Companion* and creator of the English Companion Ning, urges teachers to embrace pop culture and the media:

> Movies, advertisements, and all other visual media are tools teachers need to use and media we must master if we are to maintain our credibility in the coming years. (p. 341)

Students can learn about the tools of filmmaking (for example, cameras, lights, and sound) and techniques (like foreshadowing, juxtaposition, and symbolism) that filmmakers use to create meaning. (See the Language of Film website, www .frankwbaker.com/language_of_film, to support teacher and student learning about the tools of filmmaking.) Students can also learn about storyboarding—a process central to all media production, from advertisements to videogames to motion pictures—that involves taking a script and creating a graphic organizer so that filming can begin. Heidi Hayes Jacobs (2010) reminds us that since young people are so engaged in video and movies, it is wise to engage them in script-writing activities, as films start out as screenplays.

I turn students (and their teachers) into filmmakers in a film literacy workshop I teach titled Storytelling Through Film. I have taught this class several times to young people at the Nickelodeon Theatre, an independent film and media center located in Columbia, South Carolina. The workshop incorporates math, science,

technology, engineering, and literature into film education. Students work coop-
eratively to create their own animation flip-books, learning in the process that
there are twenty-four frames per second in film—a good math activity. They learn
that watching film involves the science principle known as "persistence of vision."
To demonstrate the process involved in film production, students read the first
two pages of the novel *Because of Winn-Dixie* by Kate DiCamillo, in which the
lead character, a little girl, discovers a dog running loose inside a grocery store.
After reading, they divide into groups to storyboard (draw) the scene they've just
read, but from a different character's point of view.

A number of apps and websites have been created to encourage film education:

- The InAWorld app allows young people to create their own movie trailers,
  which is an exercise in writing persuasive text.

- The PixStop app, created by the National Film Board of Canada, allows
  students to make their own short stop-motion films—animation produced by arranging real objects, taking a picture of them, repositioning
  the objects minutely, and then taking another picture of them to create a
  sequence of consecutive images that create the illusion of motion.

- The Storyboard Generator app, from the Australian Centre for the Moving Image, allows students to upload their own image or to use one from
  a vast image library.

- The Tate Movie Project, from the United Kingdom, involves young people in the entire movie-making process online—from hand-drawn characters and plot twists to sound effects. Students visit the website (www
  .tatemovie.co.uk) to upload their ideas and drawings and to interact with
  the film's production team. The site is constantly updated to reflect the
  students' collaborative work.

Using Advertising in the Curriculum

Nowhere is media literacy more relevant than in advertising. Advertising exists
everywhere, and advertisers are constantly devising new techniques to get and keep
our attention. Two news stories explored the lengths advertisers are now going to
engage us. One report describes how at bus stops in the United Kingdom, riders
are encouraged to push a button embedded in an ad to trigger the aroma of bak-
ing potatoes to release into the air (Metcalfe, 2012). Another report reveals that a
kind of billboard with a built-in camera uses facial recognition to target its message
only to females ("Advertising to Women," 2012). In the 2002 film *Minority Report*,
Tom Cruise portrays detective John Anderton in the year 2054. As John makes his
escape through a mall, eye-scanning billboards call him by name and invite him
to try the product. The future, it seems, is already here.

There are multiple opportunities to bring advertisements into the classroom. Not only can students conduct analyses of ads, but they can create ads as well. Media educators worldwide acknowledge that it is analysis plus production that makes for good media literacy practice. For example, during the holidays, teachers can conduct workshops around toy commercials and how they influence young people. During Academy Awards time, teachers can examine the film industry's "For Your Consideration" promotional ads. During election time, politicians' thirty-second commercials are perfect for analysis and deconstruction. See my Media Literacy Clearinghouse website (www.frankwbaker.com/default1.htm) for a list of readings, resources, and activities related to advertisement analysis.

In English language arts, advertising is useful when studying persuasion and influence. In social studies, students study the role of media in politics, the rise of advertising throughout history, and propaganda. In health classes, advertising provides material for teachers to use when considering influences on student decision making. Many students study tobacco ads from magazines as one way to understand techniques of persuasion, symbolism, and more. In art, students study the techniques (color, design, and layout) used to create marketing messages.

When I introduce advertising, I ask my students to first think as if they were advertisers. Imagine that you have a product to sell. Here are some of the questions to consider:

- Who is my audience?
- What do audience members know about my product? What do I want them to know?
- What technology or media do they read, listen to, or watch? How can I position my ad so my audience will be exposed to my message?
- What event or person can I associate the product with—a celebrity or high-profile event (such as the Super Bowl or the Academy Awards, for example)?
- What techniques will get my audience's attention (such as a blinking ad online or a digital billboard in a high-traffic area)?
- What will it cost me to advertise? Is that purchase cost-effective?
- Can I get my product featured (product placement) inside the plot of a television show or movie or on the hood of a race car?
- What incentives (such as discount coupons) can I use?
- What medium is the most effective for my message?
- How can I get people to purchase what I'm selling?

Because advertising exists everywhere, it's easy for teachers to grab an ad from a magazine or download a commercial. Since most students have not been taught how to "read" an ad, teachers will need to spend some time introducing analysis and deconstruction. My advice for teachers using print ads is to ask students to:

- Read every word on the page, even words in the smallest possible font, making note of any words with a definition they don't know

- Make a list of every image on the page, being as descriptive and specific as possible

- Make note of the techniques the advertiser has used, such as color, design, layout, font size, and style

One middle school teacher, Dianne Aldridge of Mineral Wells Junior High School in Mineral Wells, Texas, discovered that using the software VoiceThread helped her sixth-grade students become more aware of ad techniques. Figure 1.4 shows how she used the software. She placed a print ad for Nike shoes in the center of the page. The small icons to the left and right of the ad represent her students. She introduces the activity by asking the question, "I wonder what you think 'a little less gravity' means? Who's the target audience?" We see her initially in a brief video in the upper left-hand corner of the screen; then, as the VoiceThread proceeds, we hear, see, or read her students' responses. Students can react by typing a response or recording an audio or video response. Anytime during their recording, they can interact with the ad by using a drawing tool to highlight or circle a portion of the ad. She calls VoiceThread a "fabulous tool" that enables her students to reach the highest level of Bloom's Taxonomy for Higher-Order Thinking (Aldridge, 2013). Visit http://travistechies.wikispaces .com/Media+Literacy+VoiceThread to watch the Nike VoiceThread.

Studying nonprint advertisements (commercials) is similar to analyzing film-making. Because students will have had little experience analyzing the ads they see on television, teachers should introduce the tools and techniques producers use, such as the following:

- Camera angles, positions, and movement

- Lighting

- Sound, including music

- Editing (postproduction), including special effects

- Set design (the location and the props)

- Actors, including their costumes, makeup, expressions, and body language

For example, when I work with younger students, I use an advertisement for Cinderella's Magical Talking Vanity. I ask students how tall they believe the vanity is based on the advertisement. They all believe it is taller than it actually is because the way the advertisement is filmed makes it virtually impossible to know or judge the true proportions of the product. In another commercial for Typhoon 2, a toy that appears to glide on water, I pause the video to explain how an underwater shot was edited in to make it appear that the toy is gliding atop the water. (Visit www.frankwbaker.com/buy_me_that to see the lesson plan that uses this commercial.) By pausing the video at the exact spot where the toy is atop the water, I explain that through the process of editing, commercial producers can recreate and photograph the water gliding toy in a studio and edit that into the commercial; thus, unsuspecting viewers are unaware of the manipulation. Toy advertising is highly deceptive. Using it in the classroom is another way to pull back the curtain and reveal media techniques that students are usually oblivious to. By introducing the language of moving images—the tools and techniques used by media makers—students become more aware and begin to understand how each is used to create or imply meaning.

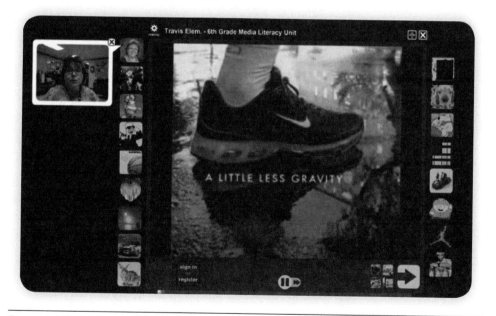

Figure 1.4: Examining a Nike advertisement using VoiceThread software.
Source: Aldridge, 2013. Reprinted courtesy of Dianne Aldridge.

For older students, once they understand the tools and techniques, they can delve deeper into commercials. They can begin to appreciate some of the symbolism common to many ads. For example, most car commercials will show the car leaving the big city and driving into the country. Car advertisers are known to use the concept of escape as its central symbolic theme to help increase the appeal of the car they are selling.

Understanding How Pictures Communicate Through Visual Literacy

In the past, visual literacy has been primarily confined to our arts classrooms where students learn how to look at a painting and learn how to read, analyze, and deconstruct the artist's techniques. Usually students study concepts such as lighting, color, composition, and more. But as business and communication expert David Gray (2008) points out:

> The three R's are no longer enough. Our world is changing fast—faster than we can keep up with our historical modes of thinking and communicating. Visual literacy—the ability to both read and write visual information; the ability to learn visually; to think and solve problems in the visual domain—will, as the information revolution evolves, become a requirement for success in business and in life.

Today, the need for visual literacy has spread to other disciplines. Because so much information is now communicated visually, it is more important than ever that students learn what it means to be visually literate in the 21st century.

A Pew survey found that 83 percent of American teens take pictures with their cell phones (Lenhart, 2010). With mobile phones and e-devices equipped with miniature cameras, it's easier than ever to take photos and upload them to an image-sharing website. In 2011, the National Board for Professional Teaching Standards (NBPTS) released the draft of its revised early childhood and middle grades reading–language arts standards, and for the first time, the organization included visual literacy:

> Reading language arts teachers know, value, and teach viewing and visual literacy as essential components of literacy instruction [that] is necessary to prepare students to interpret and interact with an increasingly visual world. (p. 3)

But taking pictures, and incorporating them into a production, is only half of the media literacy equation; teachers must also engage students in image analysis. An image in the morning's newspaper or from a textbook or a magazine is a perfect place to get started. Here is an example: Actress Jennifer Lawrence found herself on the cover of many magazines when the film *The Hunger Games* hit movie screens in the spring of 2012. I pulled three magazine cover images from the web—from *Seventeen*, *Glamour*, and *Rolling Stone*—and created a compare-contrast activity with some visual and media-literacy questions:

- Who is the audience for each publication? What are the clues?

- What are one or two adjectives to describe how she looks on each cover?

- How and what might her body language communicate?

- How are words, color, design, and layout used to make each cover appealing or attractive?

- How is each cover like an advertisement? What makes us want to pick it up, buy it, and read it?

- What are some other observations you have about the covers?

These questions, and this type of analysis, call student attention to the techniques being used by magazine cover designers and illustrators not only to make the periodical attractive but also to encourage consumers to buy it.

Software programs, such as Flickr Notes and BubbleSnaps, allow educators to embed words inside images. Figure 1.5 shows an example.

Created with Flickr Notes   Created with BubbleSnaps

Figure 1.5: "The Home of a Rebel Sharpshooter" Civil War–era photo with questions for students.

Source: Photograph by Alexander Gardner, July 1863.

I use the photo in figure 1.5, taken during the Civil War, to engage students in visual literacy. With no caption, they don't have any background, so I urge them to ask questions in order to gain knowledge. For example, they might ask:

- Who took the picture?

- Where was it taken?

- Where was it published or seen?

- What war or battle was taking place?

- Is the soldier dead?

- How did his gun get there?

As you can see from figure 1.5, I embed prompting questions to initiate student discussion. The photo in question, "The Home of a Rebel Sharpshooter," involved some manipulation, but students don't know that. It's been well documented that Civil War–era photographers who came upon battlefield scenes set up their cameras and tripods, looked through the viewfinder, and frequently did not like the composition of the bodies on the battlefield; so they moved the bodies in order to improve the composition. In the case of the rebel sharpshooter image, the photographer, Alexander Gardner, actually moved the soldier's body from the Gettysburg battlefield to this location and propped the soldier's gun up against the cave wall. After students have exhausted their questions, they will invariably want to know why the photographer moved the body. There are various answers to this question. Specifically, I want them to know that in the 1860s, people believed images represented reality—they did not question a photo's veracity; they believed everything that was in a photograph.

Today, with Photoshop and other image-altering software programs, it's easier than ever to change an image. But when is it proper to alter an image? This question is at the heart of photojournalism and popular culture today, and students should be encouraged to investigate the issue. (See www.frankwbaker.com /lesson_plan_is_seeing_believing.htm for more on "The Home of a Rebel Sharpshooter," other images, and how to use them in instruction.)

Studying Stagecraft in the Political Arena

Nowhere is visual literacy more important than in today's political world. Our endless twenty-four-hour news cycle means that the media—both formal and informal—need more and more to write about than ever before, and news can be manipulated before being transmitted to consumers and voters.

The political arena has borrowed the terms *stagecraft* and *choreography* from the world of theater, implying the need to arrange media to communicate a coherent message to an audience within the image-driven world of politics. Hundreds of people are routinely employed to manage everything from what a candidate wears, to what colors and symbols appear around him or her, to what music is playing at events. These people know that to be in charge of the image is to control what the audience sees, hears, and understands—to show members the good stuff while making it look both appealing and attractive. It's a lot like advertising, which similarly makes products look polished and bright.

Yes, candidates are like products: they are packaged and sold. In 1956, Adlai Stevenson thought this was undignified and refused to be manipulated by the admen; he lost the election to Dwight D. Eisenhower. Josh King, a former White House image expert, takes credit for creating the word *polioptics* to describe how important it is to control the image in today's media world—from giving a speech at a podium to kissing a baby at a rally.

Visual literacy requires that we all become more aware of how media messages are created, and sometimes staged, and how important it is to read what is happening (and what is not) in an image. For example, when I show the image in figure 1.6, I first ask teachers and students, "What do you see?" Invariably they say, "President Obama with doctors." I have stripped away the caption, so there is no context, and that's on purpose: I want teachers and students to look deeply at the image and consider visual literacy.

Figure 1.6: President Obama at the White House.
Source: The White House, 2009.

I ask, "How do we know they are doctors?" Students and teachers generally answer, "They are wearing white lab coats." I ask, "Do you think they arrived at the White House wearing those coats, or did the White House distribute them?"

The answer is, "We don't know—we weren't there to witness the event." But news consumers depend on photojournalists to document and report on news events. In this particular case, the White House invitation to the physicians requested they wear their white lab coats. But, in a news story critical of this photo op, one New York newspaper displayed a photo of a White House staffer handing a coat to a doctor who neglected to bring his own. So, what do you think the White House was trying to communicate via this image? Perhaps it wanted to convey that all doctors support the president's health care reform legislation, when, in fact, not all doctors do.

Photography was a new invention when Abraham Lincoln ran for president. Yet the man from Illinois posed in Mathew Brady's photographic studio several times. Brady knew how to make Lincoln look good: he raised Lincoln's shirt collar in order to de-emphasize the candidate's neck. Later, it was one of those Brady photos of "honest Abe" that some say helped get him elected.

When Franklin Roosevelt was president of the United States from 1933 to 1945, photographers agreed not to show the chief executive in a wheelchair or with crutches (he had suffered from polio). If you think about the various photos of FDR, often he was seated or standing—none showed his disability. Of the more than thirty-five thousand photos taken during his presidency, only a handful showed his disability. Controlling how the public, and the world, saw the president was paramount—and the White House did not want to give the impression that he was weak. Thus began the sometimes cozy relationship between the White House and the Fourth Estate.

One example of stagecraft comes from President Ronald Reagan's time in office. Reagan's chief image-maker, Michael Deaver, recalled the time Reagan campaigned in California at a B-1 Bomber assembly plant facing huge layoffs. Deaver, wanting to counter the idea that Reagan was a hawk (that he would be more likely to get the United States into a war), managed to have the plane strategically placed behind the president's podium, draped with a banner that declared "Prepared for Peace." With the White House dictating where all of the cameras would be positioned, the media all got the same shot: Reagan in the foreground, with the word *Peace* clearly visible in the background (Associated Press, 2007). Thus, the White House wanted to create the impression that Reagan was more interested in peace than war.

When President George W. Bush declared (prematurely) that major combat operations in Iraq had ended, with a huge "Mission Accomplished" banner hanging behind him, as seen in figure 1.7, his image-makers decided that the president should speak just as the sun was setting—creating what photographers know as the "golden hour" just before sunset. Thus, no television lights had to be used—Mother Nature would do the rest, adding to the mood and tone of the moment and making the chief executive look natural.

Figure 1.7: President George W. Bush aboard the USS *Abraham Lincoln*.
Source: Sehgal, 2011, AP Photo/J. Scott Applewhite. Reprinted with permission.

Today, when President Barack Obama goes out on the road to speak, the background most often includes an audience specially selected by the White House Office of Communications to represent an ethnically and gender diverse group, like the one in figure 1.8 (page 24).

Sometimes, stagecraft backfires. When presumptive republican presidential nominee Mitt Romney delivered a major economic speech in Detroit, Michigan, in February 2012, the location was Detroit's Ford Field, home of the professional football team the Detroit Lions. Some in the media observed that the stadium was empty—the 1,200 people in attendance actually appeared smaller when seen against the backdrop of an eighty-thousand seat arena. Was Romney's message lost from the stagecraft? Perhaps.

The following ideas for the classroom are intended to get educators and students to think about the role of visual literacy in the political arena:

- Ask students to locate and select a photo from the website of a candidate running for local, regional, or national office. If students cannot locate photos there, they should look for images on the websites of local newspapers or political blogs that cover candidates and elections. They can work in groups, with each group analyzing one photo, or students can choose a photo to analyze individually.

Figure 1.8: President Barack Obama concludes remarks on the American Jobs Act at West Wilkes High School in Millers Creek, North Carolina, on October 17, 2011.
Source: Souza, 2011.

- Since many students won't have prior experience in reading a photo, print out and distribute the Photo Analysis Worksheet created by the National Archives (www.archives.gov/education/lessons/worksheets/photo .html). This worksheet asks students to do a close-reading analysis—something called for in the Common Core State Standards. Students look for clues in the image by dividing it into quadrants and then make inferences based on what they see. Give students time to complete the worksheet and then ask them to present their observations to the class.

- If possible, invite a photojournalist into your class to discuss the challenges of covering a candidate on a daily basis. Photojournalists are our eyes and ears at events close to home and around the world. They can talk about the challenges of their jobs, whether they cover the county fair or soldiers at war. They not only take and deliver images to their organizations, but they also write the captions—something students can do as well.

See the resources collected at www.frankwbaker.com/vis_lit.htm for more about visual literacy. See my website www.frankwbaker.com/media_politics for more about the role of media in politics.

Conclusion

Many of today's educators don't appreciate how popular culture and the media can enhance instruction. Advertisements, television shows, the cover of an entertainment magazine, and a movie poster—all of these are texts designed to be read and analyzed. Today, how we read and how we watch are more important than ever. Those who don't question the media they consume are likely to become victims of advertisers, politicians, hucksters, and more.

One of the reasons media literacy education does not flourish is, for the most part, it's not taught in the United States in colleges of education, so teachers enter the workforce unprepared to deal with media or media literacy. At the same time, many of today's K–12 schools refuse to allow students to use mobile phones inside school buildings—an unfortunate and misguided regulation. I predict that the phone, just like the tablet, will become an essential instructional tool in the very near future. It is my hope that if you are reading this, and your district or school is not already teaching what I've discussed here, you will explore how to make media literacy a part of your classroom or your staff's next professional development opportunity.

References and Resources

Advertising to women: The surprising things marketers know about you. (2012, February 23). Accessed at www.huffingtonpost.com/2012/02/23/advertising-to -women-the-_n_1297974.html on May 12, 2013.

Aldridge, D. (2013). *Media literacy VoiceThread*. Accessed at http://travistechies.wiki spaces.com/Media+Literacy+VoiceThread on August 17, 2013.

Associated Press. (2007, August 19). *Longtime Reagan adviser Michael Deaver dies from cancer*. Accessed at www.foxnews.com/story/0,2933,293704,00.html on May 12, 2013.

Baker, F. (2006). *Is seeing believing? Resources for teaching about the manipulation of photographic images*. Accessed at www.frankwbaker.com/isb.htm on May 30, 2013.

Baker, F. (2007). *The role of media in elections: Helping students understand media's influence*. Accessed at www.frankwbaker.com/media_politics on May 8, 2013.

Baker, F. W. (2009). *Political campaigns and political advertising: A media literacy guide*. Santa Barbara, CA: Greenwood Press.

Beach, R., & Baker, F. W. (2011). Why core standards must embrace media literacy. *Education Week, 36*(30). Accessed at www.edweek.org/ew/articles/2011/06 /22/36baker.h30.html?tkn=NXUF6fsl2sdr2WJZryAX%2Fs6UiQssQaxXguoi&c mp=ENL-EU-VIEWS1 on May 12, 2013.

Burke, J. (2012). *The English teacher's companion: A completely new guide to classroom, curriculum, and the profession* (4th ed.). Portsmouth, NH: Heinemann.

Center for Media Literacy. (n.d.). *CML's questions/TIPS (Q/TIPS)*. Los Angeles: Center for Media Literacy.

Center for Media Literacy. (2011). *Five key questions form foundation for media inquiry: Keywords and guiding questions help build habits of critical thinking*. Accessed at www.medialit.org/reading-room/five-key-questions-form-foundation-media -inquiry on May 12, 2013.

Christel, M. T., & Sullivan, S. (Eds.). (2007). *Lesson plans for creating media-rich classrooms*. Urbana, IL: National Council of Teachers of English.

Christel, M. T., & Sullivan, S. (Eds.). (2010). *Lesson plans for developing digital literacies*. Urbana, IL: National Council of Teachers of English.

Churches, A. (2008, April 1). *Bloom's Taxonomy blooms digitally*. Accessed at www.techlearning.com/article/44988 on May 30, 2011.

Daley, E. (2003). Expanding the concept of literacy. *EDUCAUSE Review, 38*(2), 33–40. Accessed at http://net.educause.edu/ir/library/pdf/erm0322.pdf on May 12, 2013.

Daly, J. (2004, September 14). *Life on the screen: Visual literacy in education*. Accessed at www.edutopia.org/lucas-visual-literacy on May 12, 2013.

EDUCAUSE Learning Initiative. (2007). *7 things you should know about . . . digital storytelling*. Accessed at http://net.educause.edu/ir/library/pdf/ELI7021.pdf on May 12, 2013.

Edwards, E. D. (2002). To be rather than to seem: Liberal education and personal growth through documentary production. *Journal of Film and Video, 53*(4), 9–19. Accessed at http://libres.uncg.edu/ir/uncg/f/E_Edwards_To_2002.pdf on May 12, 2013.

Falcone, M. (2012, February 24). *Mitt Romney's Ford Field fumble?* Accessed at http://abcnews.go.com/blogs/politics/2012/02/mitt-romneys-ford-field-fumble on June 4, 2013.

Gray, D. (2008, May 22). *Why PowerPoint rules the business world: A call for visual literacy* [Web log post]. Accessed at www.davegrayinfo.com/2008/05/22/why-power point-rules-the-business-world on May 12, 2013.

Guernsey, L. (2011, October 25). *Screen time, young kids and literacy: New data begs questions*. Accessed at www.huffingtonpost.com/lisa-guernsey/kids-media -consumption_b_1029945.html on May 12, 2013.

Jacobs, H. H. (2010). Upgrading content: Provocation, invigoration, and replacement. In H. H. Jacobs (Ed.), *Curriculum 21: Essential education for a changing world* (pp. 30–59). Alexandria, VA: Association for Supervision and Curriculum Development.

Kilbourne, J. (1999). *Deadly persuasion: Why women and girls must fight the addictive power of advertising.* New York: Free Press.

Kubey, R., & Baker, F. (1999). Has media literacy found a curricular foothold? *Education Week, 19*(9), 56.

Lenhart, A. (2010, April 20). *Press release: Teens and mobile phones.* Accessed at www.pewinternet.org/Press-Releases/2010/Teens-and-Mobile-Phones.aspx on May 12, 2013.

Lochhead, C. (2008, August 22). Selling candidates' brand is crucial to wooing voters. *San Francisco Chronicle.* Accessed at www.sfgate.com/cgi-bin/article.cgi?f=/c/a/2008/08/21/MNAG12ES4B.DTL&type=politics on May 12, 2013.

Mehegan, D. (2007, November 19). Young people reading a lot less: Report laments the social costs. *The Boston Globe.* Accessed at www.boston.com/news/nation/articles/2007/11/19/young_people_reading_a_lot_less/?page=full on May 12, 2013.

Metcalfe, J. (2012, February 9). Inside smellvertising, the scented advertising tactic coming soon to a city near you. *The Atlantic Cities.* Accessed at www.theatlanticcities.com/design/2012/02/inside-smellvertising-scented-advertising-tactic-coming-bus-stop-near-you/1181 on May 12, 2013.

Morrell, E. (2004). *Linking literacy and popular culture: Finding connections for lifelong learning.* Norwood, MA: Christopher-Gordon.

National Association for Media Literacy Education. (2009). *Key questions to ask when analyzing media messages.* Accessed at http://namle.net/wp-content/uploads/2009/09/NAMLEKeyQuestions0708.pdf on May 30, 2013.

National Board for Professional Teaching Standards. (2012). *Literacy: Reading/language arts standards* (2nd ed.). Accessed at www.nbpts.org/sites/default/files/documents/certificates/nbpts-certificate-emc-lrla-standards.pdf on July 8, 2013.

National Governors Association Center for Best Practices & Council of Chief State School Officers. (2010). *Common Core State Standards for English language arts & literacy in history/social studies, science, and technical subjects.* Washington, DC: Authors. Accessed at www.corestandards.org/assets/CCSSI_ELA%20Standards.pdf on August 17, 2013.

Partnership for 21st Century Skills. (n.d.). *Overview: Media literacy.* Accessed at www.p21.org/index.php?option=com_content&task=view&id=349&Itemid=120 on May 12, 2013.

PS 124 Class 4-302. (n.d.). *YOU! A PSA on global warming from PS 124* [Video file]. Accessed at http://blip.tv/the-media-spot/you-a-psa-on-global-warming-from-ps-124-2713667 on July 8, 2013.

Sehgal, U. (2011, May 1). Eight years ago, Bush declared "mission accomplished" in Iraq. *The Atlantic Wire*. Accessed at www.theatlanticwire.com/national/2011/05 /mission-accomplished-speech/37226 on June 4, 2013.

Souza, P. (2011, Oct. 17). *President Barack Obama concludes remarks on the American Jobs Act at West Wilkes High School in Millers Creek, N.C.* [Official White House photo]. Accessed at www.whitehouse.gov/blog/2011/10/21/mlk-memorial-jobs-act -bus-tour-and-citizens-medal-deputies-download on August 17, 2013.

The White House. (2009, October 5). *President Obama hosts doctors for health reform* [Video file]. Accessed at www.youtube.com/watch?v=AL4VuOdKzsc on June 4, 2013.

The White House. (2011). *American Jobs Act bus tour*. Accessed at www.whitehouse .gov/photos-and-video/photogallery/american-jobs-act-bus-tour on June 4, 2013.

Travis Techies. (2013). *Media literacy VoiceThread: Media literacy takes off at Travis!* Accessed at http://travistechies.wikispaces.com/Media+Literacy+VoiceThread on May 12, 2013.

Emily Keating, MA, is the director of education at the Jacob Burns Film Center (JBFC) in Pleasantville, New York. She has overseen the development, implementation, and expansion of all of the education programs at the JBFC since their inception in September 2001. The center serves over 15,000 students a year.

Emily has worked nationally consulting nonprofit film centers on the development of their school programs and licensing and replicating curricula. She has presented on the imperative of redefining literacy in the 21st century at conferences hosted by the New Media Consortium, MacArthur Foundation's Digital Media and Learning Research Hub, the National Association for Media Literacy Education, and the Northeast Media Literacy Conference, among others. She is also an adjunct faculty member in the literacy department in the School of Education at Pace University, where she teaches Writing Process and Media Production and Literature and Digital Storytelling.

She graduated from the University of Virginia with a bachelor's degree in English language and literature and a focus in film studies and received a master's degree in education, communication, and technology from New York University's Steinhardt School of Education.

Holen Sabrina Kahn, MFA, is a filmmaker, editor, and educator. As director for educational innovation at the JBFC, she collaborated on creating curriculum for K–12 and adult education that redefines literacy in the 21st century. Previous to her work with JBFC, she taught film production, theory, and history as faculty at the City University of New York, College of Staten Island and the University of California, San Diego.

An award-winning filmmaker, Holen's work spans multiple forms including experimental, site-specific, and documentary works. Since 1998, she has collaborated with Spanish filmmaker Alessandra Zeka to produce human-rights-based documentary films, including the internationally screened and distributed *Te Dürosh* about three generations of women in Albania and *Harsh Beauty* about transgendered communities in India. She is currently codirecting and producing the feature documentary *A Quiet Inquisition*.

Holen's work has been supported by the New York State Council on the Arts, Chicken & Egg Pictures, the Jerome Foundation, New York Foundation for the Arts, the Sundance Institute Documentary Fund, and the Virginia Center for the Creative Arts. She holds a master's of fine arts from the School of the Art Institute of Chicago, was a studio fellow at the Whitney Museum of American Art's Independent Study program, and a fellow in the Genocide Studies Program at Yale University's MacMillan Center for International and Area Studies.

To book Emily or Holen for professional development, contact pd@solution-tree.com.

Chapter 2

Building a Framework for Literacy in a Visual Culture

By Emily Keating and Holen Sabrina Kahn

Educational policymakers and practitioners are increasingly recognizing the importance of integrating media and technology into the classroom. Mobile devices, tablets, and web-based platforms are making access to production tools evermore available and intuitive. Furthermore, we are progressing toward widespread support for preparing students to be technologically equipped for a workplace and culture that is visually saturated and globally connected. We celebrate this progress toward 21st century skills, yet we recognize that the foundation for student competency in these areas is still lacking. Too often, engagement in and assessment of multimedia projects still stem solely from traditional language arts skills, are based on software mastery, or are nonexistent. Just as we now recognize that a word-processed document with colorful fonts and a fancy typeface does not indicate a thoughtfully composed argument, we similarly need to unpack students' media projects that are filled with flashy transitions and preloaded effects. This chapter will go beneath the surface of media to introduce a framework for developing learners who are literate and fluent in the language of image, sound, and story.

The Jacob Burns Film Center

Just north of New York City, in the cozy commuter village of Pleasantville, is the Jacob Burns Film Center (JBFC). The nonprofit organization operates in three locations, all of which opened between 2001 and 2010: the Theater, a three-screen art house; the Media Arts Lab; and the Residence for International Filmmakers.

During its first decade of work, the JBFC has had a profound impact on advocacy for and integration of visual communication into learning environments.

The center of research at JBFC is the Media Arts Lab, a 27,000-square-foot building that features a soundstage, a recording studio, an animation studio, editing suites, classrooms, and a screening room. Visitors to this educationally dedicated facility often remark at the juxtaposition of a projector illuminating digita-editing software with whiteboard dry-erase walls and paper and pencils strewn on tables in the classrooms. High-end technology meets analog learning in a space where educators develop, pilot, and hone curricula. Programs are housed at the lab and include courses for kids, teens, and adults, as well as activities that extend beyond Pleasantville into after-school programs, social service agencies, correctional facilities, and most critically, public school classrooms. The curriculum offers a range of models, from residencies, professional development, and field trips to school partnerships. This chapter will draw from our extensive experience working with thousands of students and educators through our work at the JBFC since 2001.

The JBFC has come of age during this time of increasing awareness of the importance of media education in schools, and the adoption of the Common Core State Standards, which more readily align its mission with mandated outcomes. While curriculum design and implementation remain a primary goal for the organization, and we recognize that grade-specific films and activities are having an impact, we are convinced now more than ever that an essential contribution to the field is a framework that articulates a learning continuum for preK–12 students. Even the most thoughtful classroom production projects being implemented by teachers emphasize product over process and consider content over form. The *Learning Framework* is a macro view of the curriculum the JBFC has created to articulate a unique and essential foundation of literacy for a visual culture.

Through a cumulative and grade-based structure, the Learning Framework scaffolds the vocabulary, concepts, creative and critical structures, and production skills for gaining this literacy. At its heart is the intention to help facilitate fluency with visual and aural communication. This language of image and sound is an ancient one, but since the invention of the photographic process and image reproduction, its primacy as a communicative force has grown. The terminology of the Learning Framework stems, in many ways, from the development of a visual system and language that has roots in painting, photography, and, most resonantly, in the rich tradition of the cinema.

Old Roots, New Relevance

Since the early 1900s, academic and artistic communities have embraced and contributed to the study of cinema as a discipline, studying the depth that film offers, its ability to convincingly collapse space and time, and the impact of camera angle and movement, performance, montage, and sound. This appreciation for the art and aesthetic of film has long been accessible to college and graduate students.

Meanwhile, the television and film industries have demanded a workforce that is technically trained in operating cameras and editing content. We must re-examine the paradox of the rarefied treatment of film as art and the pragmatic need for vocational training. The revolution in mass consumption of visual media since the mid-1990s requires that everyone possess the vocabulary and understanding to read visual media. The new *media ecology* (Jenkins, 2006) reflects the convergence of multiple forms of content and the ways in which they overlap and reinvent one another. We also recognize in this term the sheer volume of content youth are consuming. The consumption as well as youth relationships to technology and sharing can be transformed into fertile ground for creative and critical participation as readers and writers of media. To enable this, it is necessary to give PreK–12 learners access to the language and literacy of the moving image.

Even as modes of production and distribution of media continue to evolve, as they undoubtedly will, the basic building blocks of this visual and aural language remain remarkably constant. As critical viewers and creators, the process of decoding meaning is still based in observing and manipulating the elements of image and sound. The very same questions can be asked of a Scorsese film and a *Sims* game: What can I see in the frame? Where is the camera? From whose point of view is the story or action unfolding? What do I hear, and how is it effecting my emotions? This decoding process can be applied to any media form. By embracing the language of cinema, we mine a medium that is part of the global consciousness and vernacular. As author and professor Vitor Reia-Baptista (2011) notes:

> The urgency to approach film, its languages and appropriations as a main vehicle of media literacy has also to do with the enormous importance of this medium in the construction of our collective memories. The richness and diversity of the film languages, techniques and technologies of film are seen as instruments of great importance, from the primitive films of Lumière and Méliès to the most sophisticated virtual inserts in YouTube.

This long and rich history has a unique language, grammar, and syntax. It includes language such as *shot*, *cut*, and *transition* and stylistic and formal elements such as composition, framing, color, and light, all of which impact meaning in a variety of ways. Just as we understand that written texts have rules and conventions that may be adhered to—or consciously broken—so too do media. Producers of all texts make choices, and those decisions impact meaning. We recognize that for students to be literate in traditional texts, they must first learn the norms of linguistic use, and, over time, we encourage them to experiment with style. The mechanics of writing are well understood, and it's accepted that students learn the proper use of capitalization and punctuation before they enter into poetics and narrative structure.

Elizabeth Daley, executive director of the Institute for Multimedia Literacy and dean of the School of Cinema-Television at the University of Southern California, put this imperative for our age succinctly in her call to action delivered at the 2002 Aspen Symposium of the Forum for the Future of Higher Education. Making the case for expanding the concept of literacy and recognizing the syntax of the visual image and its multimedia use, she states:

1. The multimedia language of the screen has become the current vernacular.

2. The multimedia language of the screen is capable of constructing complex meanings independent of text.

3. The multimedia language of the screen enables modes of thought, ways of communicating and conducting research, and methods of publication and teaching that are essentially different from those of text.

4. Those who are truly literate in the twenty-first century will be those who learn to both read and write the multimedia language of the screen.

(Daley, 2003, pp. 33–34)

The Learning Framework

Media technology trends and use change rapidly, yet the fundamental processes of comprehension and creation are based in the same language of camera, editing, sound, light, and story previously mentioned. Within this landscape, though, we recognize that terms such as *media* and *text* have become complicated and complex. The Learning Framework refers to a *text* as anything that is expressed as an image or sound, including photographs, illustrations, paintings, films, videos, digital productions, web-based material, video games, and interactive works. *Media* refers to the actual medium that the story has been constructed in, such as animation, live-performance footage, and interview footage. *Media* can also mean the news media: print, radio, television, and the web. As visual culture evolves, and the list grows, the words *text* and *media* encompass old, new, and emerging forms and use.

The most fundamental demarcation in the Learning Framework is that of *viewing and creating*—the idea that students are both readers and writers of media. In the vernacular of the JBFC curriculum, we refer to this duality as *viewing and doing. Viewing* supports close observation, discussion, and response for thinking critically, empathically, and creatively about media and its associated texts. *Creating* supports the creativity, experimentation, and deep learning that accompany the hands-on process of making. Just as we understand one would never teach reading without teaching writing, or speaking without listening, the thoughtful integration of viewing *and* representing with images is an essential pathway to literacy.

Both viewing and creating are further broken down into three stages. The phases of viewing are observation, comprehension, and analysis. The phases of creating are imagination, intention, and production. Together, they work toward decoding what is explicit or viewable in the text, what is nonexplicit or rendered invisible in the text and must be researched or garnered from outside the text, and what is brought to the text through the subjective experience of the viewer.

The framework is cumulative, with six stages of progression, from beginner to advanced—a structure that can be overlaid on a preK–12 continuum. Each section of viewing and creating is introduced with a group of overarching learning outcomes and concepts for that particular developmental stage, which address components of visual storytelling, global connections, perspective, context, structure, and the subjectivity of the viewer. There are also learning objectives, including visual language and vocabulary, such as composition, editing, and aesthetics.

Viewing

The skills and techniques articulated in the viewing component of the Learning Framework place an emphasis on deep observation, meaning making, and interpretation. As students progress, they continue to see more deeply, and they develop their aptitude for connecting form and content, understanding that texts are a collection of choices.

Observation

When one sits down to watch a film or music video, listen to a podcast, or play a video game, one's experience of viewing and listening organically engages the senses. Conventional modes of editing have evolved to make the act of viewing or listening seamless, rendering its artifice and structure essentially invisible. Breaking down the process of how one experiences and identifies visual and aural material helps narrow the focus and increase the depth of reception in small chunks. The simple question of "What can I see and hear in the text?" begins a basic practice of looking closely. It helps the learner acquire and apply new vocabulary and conceptual language, and it improves articulation and understanding of the grammar and syntax of the language. This step is essential and often overlooked. It is the first step in making the language of media transparent. Observation encompasses composition, sound design, and story elements to help bring to the surface all the elements of a text.

Providing a scaffolded learning experience is essential to the framework and to the development of a learner's visual literacy. The act of observation on the preK level can be as straightforward as noticing and identifying colors, shapes, and sounds. In the middle school years, observation begins to include camera movement, editing decisions, and visual motifs. No matter how difficult a text is, it can be approached with the basic questions of what is visible and audible. As students progress, this deep viewing should become more natural and habitual, allowing them to enter the more challenging space of how what they see and hear is interacting with the implicit and less-visible aspects of the text.

Comprehension

Whereas observation enables language acquisition, vocabulary development, and a more acute sense of looking and listening, comprehension moves the learner into a deeper exploration of "What's happening in the text?" Comprehension focuses on the ability to break down the story, plot, action, subjects, characters, and structure. This phase focuses on understanding and begins to explore how meaning is being made via the interaction of form, structure, story, and action. At an early age, students learn about basic plot structure and character development. More sophisticated applications of comprehension include foreshadowing and nonlinear concepts of time.

Analysis

The goals of practicing observation and comprehension are, in part, to support analysis. Analysis explores "What's *really* going on in the text?" It can begin on the preK level with questions as simple as "Does the story have a moral?" and grow to encompass questions as complex as "How is the camera used to frame cultural subjectivity?" Analysis draws attention to such areas as perspective, tone, intention, style, and the context in which a text was made or shown. Analysis is also where a student can explore the way bias or personal associations and experiences impact the viewing experience. At its core, analysis is the uncovering of the combined effect of all the elements that influence the meaning and subtext of a text.

The three phases of viewing merge through the student's viewing or listening experience. A learner does not suspend his or her ability to analyze what the intention of the main character is while observing where the character is in the frame or what time of day it is in the scene. Yet by focusing attention on each specific detail through questions and explorations, learners hone their eyes, ears, and mind to see the whole more clearly.

In the JBFC's third-grade program See Hear Feel Film, third graders watch an eight-minute segment from Iranian filmmaker Majid Majidi's *The Color of Paradise*. The learning outcomes are ambitious, including expanding cultural understanding, observing how feelings can be communicated without words, learning how obstacles in a story can create conflict, and experiencing empathy. To unravel these large concepts, the students watch the excerpt twice. In the first viewing, they listen closely and try to hear what the protagonist, Mohammad, a young blind boy, hears. This provides a twofold entry into the film. It enables the students to grasp how sound is impacting Mohammad's action and environment but also to empathize with him by using the same sense that he relies on. In this viewing, the students also try to figure out what Mohammad wants and what obstacles are in his way. In the second viewing, the questions they are asked focus more on the filmmaker's choices of shots. They learn to identify a long shot, a medium shot, and an extreme close-up, which helps them understand what's happening emotionally in the story. Through these two viewings, this process of observation, comprehension, and analysis work both discreetly and in tandem. By the end, students are able to better articulate the ways in which what they see and hear relate not only the story and how the character feels but also how they feel watching it.

This same process scaffolds across developmental phases and can be understood at a more sophisticated level through workshops like JBFC's Power of Persuasion, where middle school students view a collection of media clips spanning from early advertisements and wartime propaganda to contemporary ad campaigns. Using those same trifold viewing skills (observation, comprehension, and analysis), they discuss what they see and hear, investigating how the cinematography, sound, editing, lighting, framing, and style of each clip is constructing certain gender or racial representations and being effectively used to sell, advocate, and persuade.

The Learning Framework also evolves nuanced relationships into singular concepts. For example, to teach how camera angles construct how a viewer understands a character, a first grader may explore the idea that characters have viewpoints by imagining him- or herself as a caterpillar. While playacting a caterpillar, students imagine what the caterpillar sees: Are they on the ground? On a blade of grass? In a tree? What do they see from each perch? They reflect on how much of their environment they can see around them and describe and make drawings of the world from that particular view. This same idea can be evolved for a group of ninth graders, where students watch the seminal scenes from *Citizen Kane* and observe how the director, Orson Welles, shows Kane's evolving grasp on power through shifting low- and high-angle shots. Then they might take this idea and apply it creatively by taking a series of images of a classmate to create differ-ent impressions of power, thus not only learning the concept of and terminology for high-angle and low-angle camera shots but also becoming adept at producing them.

Creating

Just as breaking down the components of viewing can provide a pathway for engaged and rigorous viewing, clear, creative, and communicative expression requires a similar process.

A media literate learner needs to be supported in the creation of all kinds of texts across multiple mediums and modalities of construction, ranging from the personally inspired to the literary to the inquiry and research based. In order to achieve this, the Learning Framework lays out a process that enables a student to conceptualize, plan, produce, complete, and share projects. It celebrates a process that is iterative through encouraging drafts, edits, reflection, and exhibition. The phases of expression are imagination, intention, and production.

Imagination

Part of the power of creative activity is mining the spark that begins an idea. Imagination is often an unconscious process, which actually warrants more ded-icated time and thought. Students often feel that they have no ideas, nothing to say, and it's important that we develop their sense of confidence and excitement in generating ideas. Prompts and provocations can encourage a learner to look inter-nally or externally to cultivate creative ideas. The Learning Framework recognizes that there are infinite ways to spark the imagination and leverages these different motivations. The types of projects students engage in become more sophisticated as students' ideas and skills mature, while supporting student-driven learning as the basis for having a real stake in the creative process.

This phase, like all the others in the framework, is cumulative, so that a source for prompting imaginative ideas in kindergarten, such as inspiration from an illustrated book or song, becomes part of the pool from which a student contin-ues to pull, even as he or she adds more urbane prompts, like historical moments, literary adaptations, and personal experience.

Intention

Intention is essential to figuring out how to bring an idea to fruition and con-sidering its impact. Intention is broken into a planning stage and sharing stage. The former asks the student to think through his or her ideas before going to production. It is when he or she would determine what medium to use and what kind of materials to gather. The planning phase might include the creation of a treatment, storyboard, rendering, script, or other outline of the project. The second stage of intention is when the student articulates the meaning he or she hopes to convey, the intended impact of the completed text, and a plan for circulation or distribution. Intention goes through iterations, reflected on at various points in the expression process, and often changes as elements in production are completed or shift.

Production

In this phase, the imagined and planned idea gets made. Construction takes many forms, for example, video production or the creation of an interactive game or building a website or a reading or performance. It is here where students gain confidence and expertise in such skills as shooting and editing and demonstrate their understanding of the elements of viewing. Particular software and hardware skills are brought to bear here as well.

This trifold process of imagination, intention, and production supports all levels and modes of media making, from the discreet building-block activity described in the *Citizen Kane* example, to a five-minute documentary on a current event in one's community, to a multipage website that examines presidential debates through the last decade.

A Lens for Learning

It's helpful to consider the lens through which the Learning Framework was created. There are four modes of learning that the JBFC sees as integral and intersecting components, all of which underscore the importance of process in these new modes of literacy. The four modalities—creative, cognitive, social-emotional, and technical—support JBFC's pedagogical approach to educating the whole child. This holistic approach not only supports deep understanding of the framework content but also encourages learners to be confident, curious, empathetic, collaborative, and innovative in all their endeavors. In the *creative realm*, students engage with and relate to the imaginative and inventive and to abstract, nonlinear, and representational thinking and expression. The creative mode of learning encompasses the ability to consider the richness of the visual and aural language with an emphasis on form and aesthetic acuity. The *cognitive functionality* focuses on the articulation of intention, conception, and reflection of a text's construction and impact. It draws attention to the conscious act of decoding meaning and analysis. *Social-emotional learning* refers to how students make meaning and express themselves through empathetic and humanistic reactions, associations, and responses. Finally, *technical skills* are those students engage in the production of media. Hardware, software, and apps are required tools for a visually literate learner, and comfort and confidence navigating modes of production must be a goal.

The balance of these four elements is a vital part of the Learning Framework's dynamic approach to learning and situates media as an absolutely essential component of education. In the stratified systems of most schools, television and video courses are treated as arts electives while higher-order thinking is for the academic content areas, and "the focus on digital tools, instead of on liberating and democratizing processes in schools, has stunted . . . the role of technology in education" (Tyner, 1998, p. 85). As for social-emotional learning, in rare cases there might be some acknowledgment of giving students "life skills." We cannot shy away from the imperative to teach students art, analysis, technology, and interpersonal skills and to recognize the power of media education to do so simultaneously.

Two metacognitive processes overlaying the Learning Framework are reflection and synthesis. *Reflection* supports how learners evaluate their own work, receive and respond to feedback from peers and mentors, and refine and iterate a project. *Synthesis* draws attention to the unique personal, emotional, and psychological experience one brings to a text and the negotiation of that subjective reading with an objective and collective understanding.

Small Steps, Large Leaps

The discrete components of the Learning Framework are best understood through a brief introduction to recommendations for pedagogy. If the Learning Framework is the *what* of visual literacy, the *how* is equally significant. "Pedagogy—how teachers teach and how students learn—is at the heart of school change and serves as the linchpin for incorporating new literacy practices into the classroom. . . . Pedagogy is the 'glue' that unites media analysis and practice" (Tyner, 1998, p. 198).

There are several key tenets of the JBFC's approach to developing learners. For example, to gain proficiency in a new language, emphasis is best placed on skill building and technique. In a traditional English language arts environment, we do not expect that third graders will be writing short stories; rather, we are interested in their acquiring knowledge about structure, setting, and characterization and use writing exercises and prompts that allow them to practice discrete techniques. Similarly, learners in a visual realm are best served by the introduction and application of vocabulary in a gradual and focused way.

A prime example can once again be found in the JBFC's third-grade curriculum *See Hear Feel Film*. One of the concepts students encounter is that the camera is a tool of the filmmaker, and the camera shows us what to see. In an eight-year-old's vernacular, we're introducing the idea of *framing*. One option would certainly be to place cameras in the hands of students and let them begin shooting. However, the curriculum takes a more foundational approach to the idea of seeing and observation. The students cut out a small square in the middle of a 3½" × 5" index card and explore their classroom by "zooming in" and "zooming out" of details they find interesting. They're asked to observe and write about what a flower petal, for example, looks like up close and then far away. How does their distance from the object change the information or the emotion?

This low-tech, high-concept exercise is reinforced through their viewing of a five-minute, animated film without dialogue called *Trompe-l'oeil* directed by Ingo Panke. As the title suggests, there is a revelatory moment when the camera zooms out and the information gained by broadening the frame impacts the entire story. By focusing on the isolated idea of what the lens sees, the students are building muscles in one particular area. Well-considered exercises will feel as complete and satisfying for a group of students as a fully produced media project and provide an attainable and effective outcome. We do not plunge emerging readers and writers into fully executed texts, so we must implement the language of visual communication in bite-sized components as well. Every concept and skill in the Learning Framework can be taught through a dynamic series of activities and viewing exercises. Complete productions have an important role to play as a way to develop excitement when a project is shared and celebrated, but they are not the primary pathways to learning.

In a preK context, JBFC's Seeing Stories curriculum introduces the concept of the frame through the idea of a puppet theater stage. Here, four-year-olds are encouraged to simply consider where characters are in relation to the audience and to each other. The goal is to simply draw attention to the idea that as puppeteers they are making decisions about what the audience will see in the frame. Again, the idea of focusing on discrete skills, concepts, and vocabulary is an essential aspect of the Learning Framework.

An additional benefit of this building-block, foundational approach is that it supports a wide range of access to technology. The gap in resources in Westchester County, the home of the JBFC, is a microcosm for the broader national crisis. Disparities between districts are pronounced, and availability of resources is widely divergent. Focusing on skills, rather than fully executed short films, can require less dependence on expensive equipment and utilize more readily available resources.

Positioning New Literacies in the PreK–12 Classroom

While we continue to innovate new approaches to learning, given that the JBFC desires to implement the ideas and curriculum of the Learning Framework in schools, we have the practical consideration of content-area positioning. We anticipate core academic subject areas remaining structured as they are now, by math, science, social studies, and English language arts, for the foreseeable future. Though these silos are limiting and isolating, JBFC respects their existence and wishes to remain relevant over utopic!

The Learning Framework is most firmly grounded in the ELA environment, where communication skills are a primary goal. Within ELA, teachers have an ease and familiarity with the dual modes of communicating: speaking and listening, reading and writing. Placing the idea of viewing and representing with images alongside the more traditional modes of expressing and receiving is a logical step. Furthermore, there are clearly many areas of intersection with regards to story and structure when we consider a broad definition of text. ELA classes are also where students can explore aesthetic and poetic elements of literature, exploring language for language's sake. In addition, this is the environment in which students are becoming critical readers, learning to decode language; it's a natural extension that they develop their keen observation in tandem.

Henry Jenkins (2009) aptly reflects that "much writing about twenty-first century literacies seems to assume that communicating through visual, digital, or audiovisual media will displace reading and writing." He and we fundamentally disagree. He goes on, "Just as the emergence of written language changed oral traditions and the emergence of printed texts changed our relationship to written language, the emergence of new digital modes of expression changes our relationship to printed texts. . . . Youths must expand their required competencies, not push aside old skills to make room for the new" (p. 60). This concept of convergence is perfectly situated in an ELA context: "Writing itself is of course also a form of visual communication" (Kress & van Leeuwen, 1996, p. 15).

We understand that the learning in ELA is applied across all the content areas. Reading and writing for science, historical research, and even practical uses such as email, letters, and blogs ask that students consider audience, voice, and tone. Similarly, the language of visual communication has functions in every period of a student's school day. How better to study and document the life cycle of a butterfly than through photographic sequencing? Or demonstrate the Pangaea drift than through stop-motion animation? While content may be the core objective in the science or social studies classroom, when infused with a grounding in visual literacy, a media project can be deeply effective in bringing the content to life.

The JBFC has collaborated with educators on many projects that take a unit of study and integrate content with visual media. For example, one dynamic second-grade teacher has had a tree study as part of her science curriculum for many years. Traditionally, students would practice research skills by observing a tree in the courtyard of their school and writing their findings over the course of three seasons. With the layering of visual communication, students now use small video cameras to film the tree and use the footage as research material. With the grounding in the Learning Framework, the students actually practice tilts and pans and consider camera angle in their shooting. Their video documentation is not a haphazard or random series of shots but, rather, represents a conscious attempt to unfold a story of a tree's shape, size, and direction. Furthermore, the students take the time to review their footage, reflect on how it matches their intentions, and in some cases, actually request to reshoot because they found their camerawork too shaky or the focus slightly soft.

In another instance, a high school social studies teacher evolved a standard research paper on an influential presidential decision into a first-person digital story. Once again, not only did the students learn how to find and compose with archival materials, a not completely unheard of practice, but they were asked to consider the impact of how a particular photograph or newspaper clipping was cropped. They analyzed how sound impacted meaning and discussed how the juxtaposition of images conveyed information. Lastly, they were asked to record and overlay their own voiceover narration, which helped them understand emotion and perspective in a first-person historical account. Assessment of their final projects reflected both traditional factual accuracy but also the more subjective and formal elements of how they delivered that information. This layering of visual literacy on subject-based content is an incredibly exciting aspect of the Learning Framework's potential.

There are also media projects in which the integration of subject matter is completely seamless and inherent to the process. An example can be found in JBFC's curriculum for fourth grade, Minds in Motion. This program teaches students how to write, sequence, storyboard, and animate a stop-motion film. Stop-motion animation, also known as stop-frame animation, is a technique in which a 2-D object or piece of artwork is moved incrementally, with individual pictures taken of each position. The series of frames are then played together as continuous sequence, creating an illusion of movement. Students practice ELA skills in their story development, focusing on character, action, sequence, and conflict. They apply math content as they go through a process of preproduction known as *motion mapping*. The students learn about frame rates and go through a step-by-step planning phase of timing out each scene and calculating how many individual pictures they will need to take based upon the frame rate they are working in.

Technology is also an important element of learning as the students use stop-motion software, such as iStopMotion or Dragonframe, to animate the scene. Through these software programs, students are exposed to the concept of media capture and editing structures that transcend particular technologies. Regardless of the content matter that an eight- and nine-year-old may dream up, be it a fantastical ghost story or allegory, the production process incorporates many disciplines and modes of learning.

The Learning Framework, Curriculum, and Assessment

Any conversation with an educator in today's classrooms reveals the reality of shrinking time and narrowing focus and requirements for evidence of alignment. In this moment of high-stakes accountability, Annual Professional Performance Review (APPR), and the Common Core, the Learning Framework is, in fact, inherently and organically an assessment rubric as well as clearly mapped to national standards. Every curricula the JBFC develops includes a unit plan and a series of lesson plans that demonstrate how the goals and objectives of the project support the Learning Framework and the Common Core. There are frequent and effective connections to the Common Core's emphasis on multimedia composition, visual texts, and intertextual connections.

The Learning Framework was always envisioned as the underlying structure for building preK–12 dynamic and project-based curricula as well as assessing the effectiveness of the curricula and student learning. Teachers are often new to this language and, in fact, are often learning side by side with their students. There is often much anxiety around how to measure these new forms, and teachers may not possess a sense of what skills scaffold on others and how they can meaningfully evaluate the work their students are doing. The Learning Framework, by laying out a rubric of concepts, skills, and knowledge that students are to become familiar and fluent with, becomes a *mirror rubric* for student assessment: the learning concepts and outcomes that begin each grade catchment provide a set of clear goals for both individual growth and collaborative experience that can be assessed through JBFC's learning model of creative, cognitive, social-emotional, and technical engagement.

Whether a residency-based, school-partnership, or classroom-teacher-led program, JBFC always begins with professional development, leading teachers through the same viewing and doing processes that their students will encounter. This not only creates a pathway to sustainable integration into schools, provides the teacher with a base sense of the labor, time, and rigor involved in the work, making the process measurable. The phases of the Learning Framework—viewing and creating—help make transparent a student's thinking and progress. Particular processes, like the planning stage of intention, enable the teacher to both see how an individual and group of students are working through their ideas and provide a space for helping them reflect before moving on to questions such as, Is the idea coherent and clear? Have they considered how it will look or sound? and Have they chosen the appropriate style for their content? This engagement with a student about his or her own progress is essential to student growth and lets students partner in the evaluation of their work.

Anne Herrington, Kevin Hodgson, and Charles Moran (2009) note that though the trends of assessment and technology development are in seeming disjunction, they can be negotiated: "The world of standardized writing assessments that privilege linear, essayist literacy, and the world of contemporary society where the ability to compose nonlinear, multimodal, and sometimes interactive texts is becoming increasingly valued" (p. 14). Evaluation models are based on an analog world of writing for traditional paper texts. However, writing in the contemporary professional workplace is often presented through hyperlinks, hypertext, and web-based arenas accompanied by video and audio. It is an imperative to evolve assessments to reflect developments in technology.

The Learning Framework represents three distinct goals and aspirations that reflect a vision for all new literacies: advocacy, action, and adoption.

1. **Advocacy:** Education stakeholders are increasingly recognizing the imperative for students to be literate in the complex multimedia culture in which they are immersed. Comprehension, analysis, and verification of facts are essential skills. There is an impressive history of media and digital literacy related to Internet safety, proper virtual protocol, and mass media distribution; however, there is no definitive work on the definitions of literacy inherent in consuming visual media. The Learning Framework offers an opportunity for educators, administrators, and policymakers to understand visual literacy as a distinct skill set and draws attention to its particular vocabulary, grammar, and conventions of meaning making. The Learning Framework provides evidence of, and support for, the educational imperative of the new literacies.

2. **Action:** The Learning Framework acts as a map for all JBFC programs, preK–12. The concepts and skills outlined on paper come alive within a curriculum that reaches more than 15,000 students every year. Existing programs, as well as new content that is developed, are all informed by the relevant and vibrant Learning Framework.

3. **Adoption:** The Learning Framework is an invitation and directive to school administrators and educators across the United States to enhance literacy instruction through the pedagogy and content of media instruction. By providing a comprehensive and integrated model for teaching literacy for a visual culture, the Learning Framework informs both the scope and sequence of how students acquire and practice literacy.

As of the writing of this chapter, the JBFC is actively designing and developing a website dedicated to the expression of the Learning Framework and curriculum and case studies demonstrating its applicability. The interactive space will include the Learning Framework in its entirety and provide a community space for educators to connect, share, and showcase the innovative work they are doing bringing visual and media literacy alive in their classrooms. Visit www.burnsfilmcenter .org to find these resources.

Conclusion

The field of media education continues to grow and develop. Organizations dedicated to youth media, such as the Global Action Project and Adobe Youth Voices and Educational Video Center, have had tremendous influence on demonstrating positive student learning and outcomes. Yet, too often, the target audiences are high school students and occasionally middle school students. Media projects as outlined by the Learning Framework must be increasingly considered for younger audiences. The predominance of production programs for teens may reflect the origins of consumer access to the modes of production, but as we have demonstrated in this chapter, that access is becoming increasingly available to young learners. Emerging readers and writers are the prime audience to begin developing visual and written textual competencies in tandem. It is exciting to imagine how the child who begins learning this language in preK and is immersed in it for the next fourteen years of his or her life, sees, communicates, and navigates the world.

In her provocative meditation on the *reading brain*, Maryanne Wolf (2007) discusses the narrative of the organization of the human brain and how it was impacted by the invention of reading only a few thousand years ago. She stipulates that it is changing before our very eyes as we witness transformations in the ways we communicate.

> The goal of reading is to go beyond the author's ideas to thoughts that are increasingly autonomous, transformative, and ultimately independent of the written text. From the child's first, halting attempts to decipher letters, the experience of reading is not so

much an end in itself as it is our best vehicle to a transformed mind, and literally and figuratively, to a changed brain. (p. 10)

Our students' brains are changing in this age of screen ubiquity in ways we do not yet fully understand. Researchers are exploring how attention span, visual acuity, and sensory stimulation are evolving and how screen time may be a contributing factor. It is our collective responsibility to be a positive, productive agent in students' cognitive development—as they mature into literate, thoughtful viewers and makers of media. The next generation is more than brain matter passively receiving and absorbing images—it is made up of our future storytellers and meaning makers.

References and Resources

Daley, E. (2003). Expanding the concept of literacy. *EDUCAUSE Review, 38*(2), 33–40. Accessed at http://net.educause.edu/ir/library/pdf/erm0322.pdf on May 12, 2013.

Herrington, A., Hodgson, K., & Moran, C. (Eds.). (2009). *Teaching the new writing: Technology, change, and assessment in the 21st-century classroom.* New York: Teachers College Press.

Jenkins, H. (2006). *Convergence culture: Where old and new media collide.* New York: NYU Press.

Jenkins, H. (2009). *Confronting the challenges of participatory culture: Media education for the 21st century.* Cambridge, MA: MIT Press.

Kress, G., & van Leeuwen, T. (1996). *Reading images: The grammar of visual design.* London: Routledge.

Reia-Baptista, V. (2011). *Do we need media education to achieve media literacy? No, not necessarily, but it may help a lot!* Accessed at www.manifestoformediaeducation.co .uk/2011/01/do-we-need-media-education-to-achieve-media-literacy-no-not -necessarily-but-it-may-help-a-lot on June 4, 2013.

Tyner, K. (1998). *Literacy in a digital world: Teaching and learning in the age of information.* Mahwah, NJ: Erlbaum.

Wolf, M. (2007). *Proust and the squid: The story and science of the reading brain.* New York: Harper Perennial.

Verneda Edwards, MS, has been an educator for thirty years, working as a teacher, elementary principal, and curriculum specialist. Her most recent experience in the area of curriculum and instruction was in the Blue Valley School District in Overland Park, Kansas, as the executive director of curriculum and instruction K–12. Verneda is currently an associate professor at Baker University in Baldwin City, Kansas. Recently, her areas of interest have focused on the use of technology in the classroom, the implementation of the Common Core, and curriculum mapping.

Kristy Sailors, MS, has been in education for twenty-five years, working as a teacher, technology facilitator, and instructional designer. She is currently the director of educational technology for the Blue Valley School District in Overland Park, Kansas. A portion of her work is to evaluate and identify technologies and tools that support classroom instruction.

To book Verneda or Kristy for professional development, contact pd@solution-tree.com.

Chapter 3

Creating New Media Rubrics: Quality Student Products for the 21st Century

By Verneda Edwards and Kristy Sailors

Technology has changed our lives. Everywhere you look, people are engaged in daily activities using some form of technology. We use a search engine to get information, rather than memorizing facts or heading to the library. We look up phone numbers and addresses online. We use our phones to pay for coffee and get directions. We send digital invitations to parties. We tweet, blog, and post status updates using a variety of social media tools. Today, there is little that we do that *does not* involve technology. There is one notable exception, however— one area in which we question how technology should be used: teaching and learning (McLeod, 2012). In John Spencer's (2012) video about technology, he states that technology won't fix education, but we can't fix education without technology; technology must become an integral part of instruction, but we must also change how we view technology in education. The focus should not be on how we use technology but instead on how we can use it to support learning for students.

Most educators understand that using technology is vital in today's educational environment, but they are unsure if students are learning critical content skills when using technology. Thus, educators need to address how technology can ensure that content learning has occurred. As stated in the college and career readiness anchor standards, part of the English language arts Common Core State Standards (National Governors Association Center for Best Practices &

Council of Chief State School Officers [NGA & CCSSO], 2010), students should "use technology, including the Internet, to produce and publish writing and to interact and collaborate with others" (R.CCR.6). Today, the application and integration of technology is expected as students convey meaning in projects they develop and design. To this end, we worked with teachers in one suburban district to create and utilize rubrics that support the learning of new technology tools as well as analyze content learning using project-based assignments. The district, Blue Valley School District, is located in Overland Park, Kansas. The district is home to 22,000 students K–12. We found, through conversations and professional development sessions, that technology often overshadowed the content needs of the course and that a balance between technology and curriculum was needed. We also discovered that the key elements in designing instruction are to create project-based assignments that are rigorous and promote higher-order thinking skills (Andrew, 2013) while utilizing technology during reinforcement of content skills, and to support student learning, teachers must adapt traditional delivery methods and allow students the freedom and flexibility to use emerging technologies when demonstrating their knowledge and mastery.

As educators, we often find it difficult to move the focus of instruction from using technology to the content and skills students must learn through an assignment. Too often in courses that include a focus on technology, the learning is about the technology tool itself. Educators need to move beyond this thinking. Technology should be an essential part of the work we see in classrooms—not the focus of the work. We must understand the intent of technology tools and how they benefit the demonstration of learning. For example, we can use a tablet to engage students with content using a specific app, but the limitations of the device might require students to use another tool to demonstrate mastery. For example, if students are unable to access the complete content using a tablet, the instructional lesson will not be successful, such as if the content is not fully functional because it uses Adobe Flash–based content. In that case, we would recommend the students utilize another tool that supports Adobe Flash.

So how do educators determine how students can effectively use technology to create quality projects to demonstrate their content learning? Educators must first define quality before they can measure evidence of learning. Typically, educators use a rubric to define quality. In education, using rubrics means to define a standard of performance for an assignment or activity (National Research Council, 1996a). Rubrics were first defined for writing assessments in the mid-1970s (Dirlam, 1980) and then used to train raters for New York State's Regents Exam in Writing by the late 1970s. Mel Grubb (1981) applied the term *rubric* to such ratings in a book advocating holistic scoring rather than developmental rubrics.

Holistic scoring is used when the instructor is evaluating the product as a whole and is not concerned about the processes used to generate the final document. *Developmental rubrics* are used to identify specific components used throughout the creation process. These rubrics evaluate individual elements compiled to form the final product. Applying developmental rubrics in the grading process allows instructors and students to evaluate and score the individual stages throughout product development, providing students with appropriate feedback for each step of the project. If we expect students to create quality that is inclusive of emerging technology tools, educators must develop clear and focused evaluation criteria to distinguish acceptable responses from unacceptable responses (Popham, 1997). The criteria will obviously vary depending on the skill involved. Robert Marzano (2000), in his book *Transforming Classroom Grading*, states that most advocates agree that rubrics help determine the levels of performance or understanding of an assignment or topic. Common rubrics are particularly important within the same discipline (Jones, 2012). Richard Jones (2012) goes on to say that "using the same rubric for a variety of assignments across the disciplines reinforces the core academics and ensures a quality performance that all students and staff understand" (p. 56).

This chapter will focus on the development and implementation of rubrics that focus on the quality of the project (from a content perspective) and measure the effective use of technology tools selected by students to showcase their work. In this chapter, we will discuss:

- How to design a rubric that focuses on the effective use and application of emerging technologies

- How students can evaluate the technology tools they might use to convey the intent of their project

- How to create rubrics that focus on the appropriate use of technology tools

- Samples of rubrics that evaluate both the quality and content of technology-embedded projects

Designing Rubrics for Emerging Technologies

Rubrics are tools that teachers and students can use to assess completed work, as well as to guide the expectations and requirements of the assignment. According to Heidi Andrade (2000), an instructional rubric is a document that describes varying levels of quality for an assignment. She points out that "all rubrics have two features in common: (1) a list of criteria, or 'what counts' in a project or assignment; and (2) gradations of quality, with descriptions of strong, middling, and problematic student work." So the topic and assignment should be complex and deep enough that the learners consider several types of criteria as they work. The rubric can also provide feedback to learners as they work to complete the assignment. Rubrics identify critical components of the work so that students and teachers can measure progress toward learning targets (Jones, 2012). A well-written rubric will allow students to measure their own progress. Rubrics are most effective when they are written in a clear, concise manner so that students understand what the desired outcome is for a specific project. The criteria need to be explicit, easy to understand, and written at the level of the student (Jones, 2012; Marzano, 2000).

When designing a rubric, there are key features about the project to consider. A rubric should have the following qualities:

- It identifies the project's outcomes or learning targets for the learner.

- It effectively describes how the project will be evaluated.

- It is written in a manner that allows students to select from a variety of technology tools while maintaining the intent of the project.

- It describes the quality of the assignment itself and evaluates the use of technology.

- It provides enough distinction between each level that students clearly see the differences. The highest level allows students to go above and beyond the intent of the project.

- It should be given to students prior to beginning the project. The teacher and students thoroughly review the rubric to ensure comprehension of the expectations and requirements of the completed project.

Evaluating Potential Technology Tools

As students make decisions about which technology tools to use, it is important for them to review the rubric that will be used to evaluate their project. By using the criteria included on the rubric, students can select a tool that will allow them to generate a completed project that aligns with the expectations of the assignment. To evaluate the tool, students will need to take the following five steps and ask the related essential questions:

1. **Evaluate the source**—Is there a cost or subscription associated with the tool? Do I need to create an account in order to use the tool? Does the tool require additional (third party) software to function?

2. **Determine accessibility and compatibility**—Is the tool web-based, does it need to be installed, and is it compatible with my computer?

3. **Determine the security and level of control**—Is the source password protected, is it stored and backed up on the web, and how does the end user obtain access to the tool?

4. **Determine ease of use**—Is the tool easily navigated, or does it require training to operate? Does the website contain helpful instructional resources such as manuals or videos?

5. **Evaluate the use for the end product**—Is the information easily obtained or archived for future access? What output does the tool produce? How will the end user access the final product?

Table 3.1 provides examples of essential questions and sample outcomes for each of the five steps.

Table 3.1: Evaluating Technology Tools

Steps	Essential Questions	Sample Outcomes
1. Evaluate the source.	• Is the tool free, or does it require payment? • Do I need to create an account prior to using the tool? • Does the tool require additional software or plug-ins?	• The vendor requires a credit card or an account. • I must have a specific plug-in (Adobe Flash, for example) in order to operate the tool.
2. Determine accessibility and compatibility.	• Do I need to download or install the tool? • Is the tool web-based? • Does the tool require a specific operating system?	• I must download and install the software before I can use it. • The tool is designed for a specific operating system, such as OS X or Windows 7.
3. Determine the security and level of control.	• Does the tool or site require a password or an account to gain access? • How do I access the tool?	• I must complete a form and create a username and password prior to accessing the tool. • The tool is available on a website. • The tool is installed on my computer.

Continued →

Steps	Essential Questions	Sample Outcomes
4. Determine ease of use.	• Is the tool easy to learn about and navigate? • Does the tool require additional training or information?	• I am required to watch tutorials or read a manual before using the tool.
5. Evaluate the use for the end product.	• What output method does the tool provide? • Can I easily obtain or archive the information for future access?	• The tool allows me to export the content in a variety of formats, such as a web address, link, or file. • The tool allows me to send access via email or with a link.

For example, a student is given a task to research the best tool to poll other students in his class. Using the steps in table 3.1, the student can conduct a search for the best tool using a standard search engine. By following the steps, the student is able to evaluate the tools he has found and select a web-based tool that meets the needs of the project.

Creating Rubrics That Focus on Technology Tools

Web 2.0 tools are online tools that go beyond the static webpage. When incorporating technology into an assignment, students must select their technology tools based on the features and functionality of the tool and how it contributes to the project, as explained in the previous section. It is important that the project is evaluated holistically and that the evaluation is inclusive of the technology used to generate the project. However, there may be times when an instructor wants to evaluate only the student's use and integration of the technology tool. This should be done toward the beginning of the project, during the phase when the students evaluate and select which tools they will use to create their project. During the initial phase of the project, it is necessary to provide students with the rubric that identifies the critical components of what will be evaluated.

It's certainly difficult for educators to keep up with the ever-changing landscape of emerging digital media. However, through research and collaboration with peers and students, teachers can stay current regarding available tools. The technology tools students can use to strengthen their projects are too numerous to mention, so in this section of the chapter, we show sample rubrics that focus on some popular tools that are available on the Internet. The following sections provide an overview of a specific tool and then provide a sample rubric to evaluate the application and use of that tool. These tools include Prezi, an online presentation program; Glogster, a blogging tool that can strengthen student writing in an authentic environment; Animoto, a tool to create and edit videos; SlideShare, a web-hosted service for posting documents and projects; and finally, tablet apps.

Prezi

Prezi is a presentation tool that uses a unique zoom feature to enhance presentations. It allows individuals to collaborate, develop, and share presentations using a variety of delivery methods. Prezi is often considered an alternative to Microsoft PowerPoint. Prezis can be shared by creating a URL that directly links others to the Prezi to allow them to access, view, or collaborate on the presentation. A feature of Prezi not included in Microsoft PowerPoint is the ability to access the presentation online and develop it collaboratively. A Prezi works well when a student is attempting to share content in a more appealing way than a traditional PowerPoint presentation. It is more difficult to develop Prezis, but they are considered more engaging because of how the program flows from one image to the next. Figure 3.1 is an example of a rubric that can be used to evaluate a project that uses Prezi.

	1	2	3	4
Use of multimedia	No multimedia sites are used in this presentation.	One multimedia site is used, but it does not flow with the presentation.	At least one multimedia site is effectively used in the presentation.	Two or more multimedia sites are used effectively in the presentation.
Content	The content does not match the intent of the message being conveyed.	The content and the message are conveyed, but the meaning isn't always understood.	The viewer understands some of the content of the presentation, but it leaves some doubt to what the learning should have been.	The viewer clearly understands the content of the presentation.
Language and grammar structure	There are a significant number of errors in spelling and sentence structure.	There are some spelling errors in the presentation and inappropriate use of sentence structure.	There are few spelling errors with some inappropriate use of sentence structure.	There are very few errors in the writing of the presentation.
Use of features	Only one feature of Prezi is used during the presentation.	Two features of Prezi are used during the presentation.	Three features of Prezi are used during the presentation.	Four or more features of Prezi are used during the presentation.

Figure 3.1: Rubric for evaluating student use of Prezi.

Glogster

Glogster is a web-based communication tool used for blogging and creating interactive posters, infographics, and files. Glogster allows users to create web-based projects that incorporate text, images, videos, weblinks, and graphics. There are many free blogging services that teachers and students can utilize for classroom instruction. Glogster provides students with a venue to communicate ideas and thoughts using the web. It is a great tool for students to document their progress and their phases of planning throughout the duration of a project. Figure 3.2 is a sample rubric for evaluating Glogster and other blogging tools.

	1	2	3	4
Writing process	Student does not use writing strategies in the project.	Student uses some writing strategies, but they are not coherent.	Student demonstrates good use of learned writing strategies and creates a coherent project.	Student demonstrates excellent use of writing strategies and creates a project that demonstrates learning.
Content	Content or purpose of the blog is not evident.	Writing touches on a couple of content areas, but the focus of the blog is unclear.	The content or purpose of the blog is understood, but it is not sustained.	There is clear purpose and understanding of the content of the blog.
Images	Student makes no use of images.	Student uses an image, but it does not match content of topic.	Student uses an image tied to the content.	Student achieves excellent use of an image that conveys the intent.
Language and grammar structure	Blog contains many errors, but the reader still understands the main idea.	Blog contains some errors but is easier to understand.	Blog is basically well written but still has some errors.	Blog is well written with very few errors.

Figure 3.2: Rubric for evaluating student use of Glogster.

Animoto

Animoto is a tool that allows the user to upload images, graphics, and audio files to create professional-looking videos. It is a great tool for students to use to visually demonstrate their mastery. Using this tool, students can create interactive presentations that include audio, images, and text, such as multimedia book reports, project summaries, and science labs. Figure 3.3 is a sample rubric for evaluating projects generated using Animoto.

	1	2	3	4
Content	All required content or elements are not identified.	The product lacks direction, and the information is not clear.	The product shares clear content, but it is not clear what the author is trying to convey.	The product shares clear content that is well thought out and thorough in its delivery.
Voice and sound	Content does not contain video or sound.	Delivery is not smooth but it holds the audience's attention a portion of the time. Narration may be difficult to hear. Voice shows little inflection. Audio is missing or distracting.	Content is rehearsed, with a fairly smooth delivery that usually holds the audience's attention. Narration is heard over the audio. Voice sounds natural and avoids monotones. Audio neither adds nor distracts from the project.	Content is interesting and well-rehearsed with smooth delivery that holds the audience's attention. It has easy-to-hear narration over the soundtrack. Voice sounds natural and helps convey meaning. Soundtrack adds to the tone and feel of the project.
Images	Images do not match the content of the project.	Some of the images convey the intent with some citations listed.	Most of the images are relevant to the subject. Majority of citations are included.	All images support the content and clearly convey the intent of the project. All citations are included and are accurate.
Presentation	Presentation does not flow in a manner that the viewer can understand.	Use of fonts, color scheme, and overall presentation of images is distracting and does not convey understanding of the content.	There is effective use of fonts (but limited wording) and appropriate organization of color scheme and graphics to help convey content.	There is excellent use of font, color scheme, and images to convey understanding of the content.
Copyright and acceptable use	Content does not follow copyright.	Content includes a few citations but contains errors.	Content includes multiple citations and references but contains errors.	Content follows all copyright guidelines and contains no errors.

Figure 3.3: Rubric for evaluating student use of Animoto.

SlideShare

SlideShare allows users to create, collaborate on, and publish presentations online. The importance of such a tool is it allows students to share their products with individuals outside of their classroom. SlideShare allows students to incorporate images, text, and video into their product and then distribute their multimedia presentations that might exceed the size limit of email. Students share their presentations by providing the weblink to the specific file. Figure 3.4 is a sample rubric for evaluating projects created using SlideShare.

Tablet Apps

Tablet-specific apps allow users to create, collaborate on, and manipulate content. There are over one million apps available through the Apple store. The Android market boasts more than 500,000 apps available for download. As consumers and educators, we must understand how to evaluate the growing number of available apps. We recommend that prior to students reviewing an app in class, the teacher should review and be aware of the app's content and age appropriateness. Students can then review the app using the criteria in a rubric. Figure 3.5 (page 60) is a sample rubric for evaluating tablet apps for both teachers and students.

Evaluating Both Content *and* Technology Tools in Student Products

In today's educational landscape, it is imperative for educators to maximize the use of assessments that provide feedback to students. The ability to evaluate the quality of a project to meet specific educational learning targets as well as monitor appropriate use of technology will better support student learning. Assessing technology use in isolation of product quality is shortsighted and could limit student growth in both areas.

Evaluating Digital Presentations

Digital presentations allow students to learn how to design and present projects using an online format. Using a digital presentation, the student conveys his or her message entirely through a web-based resource. Content included in digital presentations should incorporate basic design fundamentals, including appropriate formatting, spacing, and relevant content. We discussed several open-source tools in the previous section that students can use to create digital presentations. When evaluating potential digital-presentation tools, the critical piece of the evaluation process is not to assess how a student uses a particular tool but how any

	1	2	3	4
Content	Content is not identified.	The product lacks direction, and the information is not clear.	The product shares clear content, but it is not clear what the author is trying to convey.	The product shares clear content that is well thought out with thorough information.
Voice and sound	Content does not contain video or sound.	Delivery is not smooth but it holds the audience's attention a portion of the time. Narration may be difficult to hear. Voice shows little inflection. Audio is missing or distracting.	Content is rehearsed, with a fairly smooth delivery that usually holds the audience's attention. Narration is heard over the audio. Voice sounds natural and avoids monotones. Audio neither adds nor distracts from the project.	Content is interesting and well-rehearsed with smooth delivery that holds the audience's attention. It has easy-to-hear narration over the soundtrack. Voice sounds natural and helps convey meaning. Soundtrack adds to the tone and feel of the project.
Images	Images do not match the content of the project.	Some of the images convey the intent of the project.	Most of the images are relevant to the content of the project.	All images support the content and clearly convey the intent of the project.
Presentation	Project does not flow in a manner the viewer can understand.	Use of fonts, color, and overall presentation of images is distracting and does not convey understanding of the content.	There is an effective use of fonts (but limited wording) and appropriate organization of color and graphics to help convey content.	There is an excellent use of font, color, and images to convey understanding of content.
Copyright and acceptable use	Content does not follow copyright.	Content includes a few citations but contains errors.	Content includes multiple citations and references but contains errors.	Content follows all copyright guidelines and contains no errors.

Figure 3.4: Rubric for evaluating student use of SlideShare.

	1	**2**	**3**
Relevance	App does not contain appropriate content.	App contains appropriate content but is not age appropriate.	App contains content that is age appropriate and educationally relevant.
Feedback	App does not provide feedback to user.	App provides minimal feedback to user.	App provides feedback based on user actions.
Engagement	User is not engaged with app.	User has minimal engagement with content of app.	User is fully engaged with content of app.
Customization	App does not provide customization option.	App provides minimal customizations.	User is able to fully customize the settings within the app.
Usability	The user is not able to launch the app without assistance.	The user is able to launch and navigate the app with minimal instruction or direction.	The user does not require assistance with the app.

Figure 3.5: Rubric for evaluating tablet apps.

web-based tool could be used to produce a quality digital presentation. When assigning students the task of creating digital presentations, emphasis should not be on what web-based tool the student used to generate the project but how the student applied visual and design elements within the project.

In preparation to create a digital presentation, students must consider who their audience will be, what the message is they are trying to convey, and if the content is accurate and relevant to their desired outcome. Another factor they must take into consideration is the delivery method for the final product. How will they present the material to the audience? What, if any, are the limitations for the end user? They could choose to deliver the content through a website, an infographic (a graphic representation of data), blog, video, or podcast. Delivery methods for digital presentations are unlimited.

How does one develop a tool to evaluate a complex project such as digital presentations? The rubric must be written so it will not limit the original intent of the work but still include the required elements of what a quality project would encompass regardless of the technology used to develop the product. A rubric designed for digital presentations is more than just a measure of the content; it also assesses the delivery method and technology used to generate the final product. Evaluating a digital presentation requires the teacher to review the delivery method as well as the content contained in the material. A sample rubric for evaluating a digital presentation is shown in figure 3.6. Unlike the earlier rubrics in this chapter, this rubric contains instructions to the student. As in all projects, the teacher should share the rubrics with students prior to beginning the design phase of the assignment. This allows students to consider all desired elements when designing the product.

Instructions to the student: *With the information you gathered on your chosen topic, create a digital presentation using a web-based tool that conveys the intended message for your assignment. Use the evaluation rubric that follows to prepare a quality presentation. Be sure to include the required elements for the project.*			
	1	**2**	**3**
Organization	Information is presented in a way that is too difficult to follow.	Information is presented in an interesting format that can be followed.	Information is presented in an interesting, sequential order that is easy to follow.
Audience	Information is designed in a format that does not meet the needs of the targeted audience and is difficult to navigate.	Information is designed for a targeted audience but is difficult to navigate.	Information is designed for a targeted audience. Users are able to successfully navigate the material.
Content	The presentation includes inaccurate information and contains more than two typographical or grammatical errors.	The presentation includes inaccurate information and contains one or two typographical or grammatical errors.	The presentation includes accurate, relevant information, uses appropriate grammar and punctuation, and follows project requirements.
Delivery	Information is presented in a format that is inaccessible by the end user.	Information is presented utilizing appropriate technologies but includes errors when accessed by the end user.	Information is presented utilizing appropriate technologies, formatting, and tools available to the end user (website, computer, and so on).

Figure 3.6: Rubric for evaluating a digital presentation.

Evaluating Digital Storytelling

Storytelling has changed. In the book *The Art of Immersion*, Frank Rose (2011) states, "The Web began its transition from a simple delivery mechanism to the cornucopia of participation (blogs, wikis, social media) known as web-based" (p. 7).

More and more people are moving to the broadband Internet, and new software tools are making it easy to build online platforms that enable people to connect.

Digital storytelling is simply telling a story using digital means, such as a website, video, podcast, or blog. It elicits the same emotions as traditional storytelling but relies solely on technology for delivery (Gottschall, 2012). Most often when an individual thinks of storytelling, he or she associates it with a fictional tale. Digital storytelling includes both fiction and nonfiction. For example, a story could be a revised version of a traditional favorite—such as Grimm's *Hansel and Gretel*—that combines the original story with cutting-edge graphics and visual effects. Or, the story could take a real event, such as a battle, and recreate it with topographical views and nonlinear content. For example, a story could include a presentation about President Lincoln and his role in the Civil War. The story could convey Lincoln's burden through visual imagery and his written word as he led the country in wartime. The possibilities are limitless.

Digital storytelling should convey strong emotions to the viewer. As Jonathan Gottschall (2012) notes, if the storyteller is skilled, he or she simply invades us and takes over. Students must harness the power of the story and convey it to the audience in their projects. For example, as the trouble in the Middle East continues to unravel and countries in that area struggle for democracy, what story needs to be told? Is it the story of an American ambassador who was killed and his journey to serve that part of the world, or is it the story of an individual rebel sacrificing his life for a chance to rid his country of a ruthless dictator? Both are powerful stories that need to be told.

To demonstrate the skills of digital storytelling, students need to be able to create presentations using several types of technologies. Consider the following criteria (Goldblatt, Rigby, Rogers, & Vergara, 2012) and how each will be incorporated into the final product. Teachers can consider these criteria when developing an evaluation rubric.

- What program (tool) did the student select, and why? Is it web-based, or is it a tool that must be installed on computer hardware?

- How is the student presenting the story to the audience? Who is the target audience?

- Is there a balance between the use of technology and the content of the story?

- What visual effects did the student use to portray the story? Did the visual and audio effects add to the story, or were they a distraction?

- What preplanning occurred? Did the student complete a storyboard? How were the characters built into the story?

- Did the student successfully collaborate with others to create a quality project?

As students begin to design their digital story, they should consult the rubric to ensure their project reflects the complexity of the skills being evaluated. The final project must be comprehensive and include all components outlined in the rubric, such as visual, audio, text, and technology tools. For example, students must decide whether written text or audio will best convey the intent of the story. Finally, the digital tools students have selected must best portray the emotion of the story and convey the message. Students should continue to review the rubric as they work on the project. As students prepare to use the rubric for determining the quality of their story, they still need to employ sound presentation techniques. For example, having riveting content will not hold the attention of the audience if the presenter chooses to sit or speak in monotone during the presentation. Likewise, if voice-over used during a presentation is overdone (for example, it is in a strange accent) and garners more attention than the story itself, the audience will not hear the message. A sample rubric for digital storytelling is shown in figure 3.7. It merges the electronic tools as well as the content and the delivery of the story.

	1	2	3
Topic	The topic is irrelevant and does not fit the targeted audience. The message is one that is not of much interest.	The topic is relevant and appropriate to the project but does not fit the targeted audience. The message is of importance.	The topic is relevant and appropriate to the project and targeted audience. The message is one that impacts others.
Research and sources	The project contains information that does not appear to be credible or cited.	The project contains information that appears to be credible but is not cited. At least two sources are used to create the project.	The sources are credible and cited. The project uses a variety of sources (traditional and web-based). The project includes at least five sources.
Audience	Information is designed in a format that does not meet the needs of the targeted audience and is difficult to navigate.	Information is designed for a targeted audience but is difficult to navigate.	Information is designed for a targeted audience. Users are able to successfully navigate the material.
Audio and visual effects	The audio and visual effects distract from the message of the story.	The project includes images that enhance the understanding of the story.	The project includes both images and videos that enhance the understanding of the story. The visual and audio effects enhance the presentation and support the story.

Figure 3.7: Rubric for evaluating digital storytelling.   Continued →

	1	2	3
Presentation (digital or traditional)	The project uses traditional delivery methods.	The project uses digital tools (computer, Internet, and so on) but does not include appropriate presentation techniques including design, color, spacing, and timing.	The project uses digital tools (computer, Internet, and so on) and appropriate presentation techniques including design, color, spacing, and timing.
Technology tool	The project must be installed on a computer in order to be viewed.	The project can be viewed using the Internet.	The project can be viewed using a variety of formats (Macintosh, PC, tablet, or smartphone).

Conclusion

Is it possible to ensure students master instructional content using emerging technologies? The short answer is yes. Student assignments can be meaningful within a content area and also effectively use technology—if teachers create and use rubrics to guide themselves and students regarding the quality of technology within tasks or projects. As one teacher we worked with put it, "For students—this [technology] is their language. They want to use it. They feel like they're in control of their learning. It's the future." It is time educators make the transition to regular technology use to engage learners in the content areas. This is a learning process for both teachers and students. With appropriate planning and implementation, students show higher levels of engagement while being more autonomous and using a variety of emerging technologies to demonstrate their comprehension and mastery. Technology rubrics support students in being able to identify, evaluate, and use online tools. Because they gain confidence with these tools, they are able to focus on the content of the product—not just on the technology portion.

New technology tools for education are emerging daily. It is difficult to keep up with the changing landscape. As online tools continue to evolve, educators and students who use rubrics will be able to research, evaluate, and select the emerging technology that best supports the desired outcome. It is not the technology tool itself that will sustain the student over the years—the tools change too rapidly. It is the learning of the content while utilizing the technology that will support academic growth.

References and Resources

Andrade, H. G. (2000). Using rubrics to promote thinking and learning. *Educational Leadership, 57*(5), 13–18.

Andrew, T. (2013, March 25). *Identifying project based assessments.* Accessed at http://suite101.com/article/identifying-project-based-assessments-a95072 on July 8, 2013.

Dirlam, D. K. (1980). Classifiers and cognitive development. In S. Modgil & C. Modgil (Eds.), *Toward a theory of psychological development* (pp. 465–498). Windsor, England: NFER.

Goldblatt, S., Rigby, B., Rogers, T., & Vergara, C. (2012, June). *Where do we go from here.* Panel conducted at the Digital Storytelling Forum, Kansas City, MO.

Gottschall, J. (2012). *The storytelling animal: How stories make us human.* Boston: Houghton-Mifflin Harcourt.

Grubb, M. (1981). *Using holistic evaluation.* Encino, CA: Glencoe.

Jones, R. (2012). *Using rigor and relevance to create effective instruction.* Rexford, NY: International Center for Leadership in Education.

Marzano, R. J. (2000). *Transforming classroom grading.* Alexandria, VA: Association for Supervision and Curriculum Development.

McLeod, S. (2012, October 14). *The ups and downs of educational technology advocacy* [Web log post]. Accessed at http://dangerouslyirrelevant.org/?s=The+ups+and+downs+of+educational+advocacy&x=0&y=0 on October 29, 2012.

National Governors Association Center for Best Practices & Council of Chief State School Officers. (2010). *Common Core State Standards for English language arts and literacy in history/social science, science, & technical subjects.* Washington, DC: Authors. Accessed at www.corestandards.org/ELA-Literacy on October 29, 2012.

National Research Council. (1996a). Assessment in science education. In *National Science Education Standards: Observe, interact, change, learn* (pp. 75–102). Washington, DC: National Academies Press.

National Research Council. (1996b). *National Science Education Standards: Observe, interact, change, learn.* Washington, DC: National Academies Press.

Popham, W. J. (1997). Special topic: What's wrong—and what's right—with rubrics. *Educational Leadership, 55*(2), 72–75.

Rose, F. (2011). *The art of immersion: How the digital generation is remaking Hollywood, Madison Avenue, and the way we tell stories.* New York: Norton.

Spencer, J. (2012, October 6). *Technology will not fix education* [Video file]. Accessed at www.educationrethink.com/2012/10/video-technology-will-not-fix-education.html on October 29, 2012.

Heidi Hayes Jacobs, EdD, is an internationally recognized expert in the fields of curriculum and instruction. She writes and consults on issues and practices pertaining to curriculum mapping, dynamic instruction, and 21st century strategic planning. She is president of Curriculum Designers and director of the Curriculum 21 Project, whose faculty provides professional development services and support to schools and education organizations. Featured prominently as a speaker at conferences, at workshops, and on webinars, Heidi is noted for her engaging, provocative, and forward-thinking presentations. She is an accomplished author, having published eleven books, journal articles, online media, and software platforms. Above all, Heidi views her profession as grounded in a K–12 perspective thanks to her early years as a high school, middle school, and elementary teacher in Utah, Massachusetts, Connecticut, and New York.

Heidi completed her doctoral work at Columbia University's Teachers College, where she studied under a national Graduate Leadership Fellowship from the U.S. Department of Education. Her master's degree is from the University of Massachusetts Amherst, and she did her undergraduate studies at the University of Utah. She is married, has two adult children, and lives in Rye, New York.

To learn more about Heidi's work, visit www.curriculum21.com and follow her on Twitter @curriculum21 and @heidihayesjacob.

Frank W. Baker is a much sought-after media literacy education consultant. He has written teaching standards and supporting documents for the state of South Carolina. He is the author of three books; his most recent is *Media Literacy in the K–12 Classroom*. He created and maintains the internationally recognized Media Literacy Clearinghouse website (www.frankwbaker.com/default1.htm), and he conducts media literacy workshops at conferences, schools, and districts across the United States. He is a former consultant to the National Council of Teachers of English and the South Carolina Writing Improvement Network.

To learn more about Frank's work, visit him on Twitter @fbaker or on his blog at www.ncte-ama.blogspot.com.

To book Heidi or Frank for professional development, contact pd@solution-tree.com.

Chapter 4
Designing a Film Study Curriculum and Canon

By Heidi Hayes Jacobs and Frank W. Baker

With fervor and ferocity, a group of high school English language arts teachers argued with the department chair over Mark Twain, Lois Lowry, and Maya Angelou until 5:00 p.m.—the coffee had long since run out, but the teachers' energy level had not; they needed to reach agreement on the literary canon. Concurrently, an elementary school staff on the other side of town debated Eric Carle, Lois Lowry, and Judy Blume with equal passion. Literature brings out that passion in teachers. From Shakespeare to Chaucer, the canon is the crucial arbiter of what we will pass on to the next generation about our knowledge of the human condition.

The word *canon*, from late Latin and Middle English, means *rule, ruler*, and *model* and can be traced to the Greek *kanon*. The use of the term certainly has historically been evident in religious practice as used, for example, in canonical references to the Bible. A work that is included in the canon, in a very real sense, becomes "canonized." Though not given sainthood, it is accorded very special attention. George P. Landow (1989), professor of English and art history at Brown University, puts it this way:

> Such an announcement of status by the poem, painting, or build-
> ing, sonata, or dance that has appeared ensconced within a canon
> serves a powerful separating purpose: it immediately stands forth,
> different, better, to be valued, loved, enjoyed. It is the wheat win-
> nowed from the chaff, the rare survivor, and it has all the privileges
> of such survival.

There is obviously no single agreed-upon canon for any culture or group. As professor John M. Bowers notes in his course Western Literary Canon in Context, throughout history to the present, when it comes to determining and wrestling with the canon, there are four main influences: editors, culture, education, and controversy (Bowers, n.d.). Indeed, the notion of a canon is often fraught with debate and tensions. Creating a canon is about making strategic choices concerning what works of literature should be requisite for student study. However, those who support student-centered curriculum models would argue that there should not be a pre-existing canon and that learners should be supported in making individual discoveries and choices. The question is often raised, Should there be a canon at all? And, then, for those who espouse a canon, the debate circles around what books should be included and which books will be left off the list. The truth is that whatever choices we make as teachers and administrators do, in fact, directly impact our learners. Students will be exposed to the works we choose. If we choose *Romeo and Juliet*, then they will read it, and it is highly unlikely most students would choose it on their own. So, if we believe that there are essential works that our learners need in order to understand who they are in the time in which they live, the traditions of the past, the nature of quality writing, and the dazzling range of human talent as inspiration, then wrestling with a canon matters. And we must consider the media as well. Different media require different though perhaps complementary skill sets. Similar questions emerge regarding exposure to core works in the world of cinema. The word *classic* appears frequently in conversation and discussion regarding film among adults, but have our students had sufficient experience with guided instruction to make determinations about classic work? Certainly the curriculum track record on film is spotty at best.

In this chapter, we hope to provide support for both the integration of formal film studies in the K–12 curriculum and the cultivation of a working film canon. To do so, we will:

- Argue the need for film study and a film canon across curriculum areas and age ranges

- Consider prominent film study models and available film resources

- Examine five instructional tenets to support film study for teachers

- Propose criteria and a procedure for creating a film canon, along with a sample canon for several grade levels

Why Study Film?

Given film is mostly a 20th century genre, it is surprising that formal study is still on the instructional periphery in the United States; we have over one hundred years of film media to consider for the curriculum. What is it about film that makes it so appealing? Why do so many of us love to sit on our couches (or theater seats) and take in the latest release? Film continues to captivate us and often becomes part of our national dialogue. Huge television audiences still gather around the tube to watch (and experience) the Academy Awards. Films are annually added to the Library of Congress's National Film Registry. The American Film Institute (AFI) produces television specials and polls audiences about film. Top-ten lists pop up every month on blogs, on websites, and in magazines. Thousands of websites are devoted to film, filmmakers, and filmmaking.

Why do some teachers use video and film in instruction and others do not? Why is there a lack of formal attention to film study in our K–12 curriculum? With the exception of an elective course or an occasional viewing of a film adapted from a book, nominal attention has been given to a formal debate or discussion of the film canon in the United States. Certainly there is support from advocacy groups. The National Council of Teachers of English (NCTE) encourages its members to teach with and about film. In 1932, NCTE created the Committee on Photoplay Appreciation, which made recommendations about film use in English classes and generated study guides for teachers (Young, Long, & Myers, 2010).

Several NCTE resolutions urge teachers to include nonprint texts in the classroom. A one-day film festival is a feature of the organization's annual teachers' convention. We applaud the spirit of the resolutions, but, proportionally, these efforts are telling: they emphasize enrichment over necessity.

Our experience in the United States is that an individual secondary school teacher might be a film buff and include some wonderful cinema experiences in his or her classes, but this informality is creating a gap in our students' education. Certainly, elementary teachers will have the opportunity to show a movie to a class, but they rarely look at film as a critical study with the same spirit they do when introducing students to literature. We have heard teachers raise a valid concern that because there is no emphasis on assessing a student's film knowledge, there is no room to integrate cinema into the curriculum. Our current standardized assessments in no way reflect student competence in media literacy.

The lack of film study in the past may be due to the expense of renting a film in a reel and having the equipment to run it in the auditorium. Clearly, with the current abundance of resources and ease of accessing film clips, a wide range of educators can and do support formal film study. Teachers, school librarians, and media arts teachers can easily acquire more titles for use in the classroom via DVDs, and websites like Movieclips make it easier than ever to incorporate film into instruction. Given this, what are the reasons for the lack of consistent and concerted attention to film study?

A groundbreaking and detailed study in the United Kingdom (British Film Institute, 2012) identifies reasons why there is a scarcity of attention to film study in the curriculum in schools and universities. There is general consensus that teachers are enthusiastic about the filmmaking process and work together to generate new ideas, but film is not part of study for the following reasons:

- It is difficult for teachers to fit film education into their curriculum because of government standards. Students are encouraged to demonstrate their learning in twenty-minute chunks, so teachers worry about using film education since films require longer blocks of time to engage students.

- Teachers at different stages of their career report a lack of confidence in using filmmaking technology. The teachers reported that a lack of support in schools perpetuated their inability to use film technology.

- Some teachers still do not regard the use of film as a reliable learning tool compared to text.

- Only a small minority of teachers value the opportunity of using simple, affordable, and easily accessible technology such as flip cams, although it was reported that some schools planned to invest in iPads for film education in 2013.

- Teachers are not able to access London film seminars and events; thus, there is a market for local training hubs and resources.

We believe these findings would likely be replicated in the United States and other developed countries and could help explain many of the reasons that film study is still often considered enrichment and hovers on the fringe of curriculum planning and instructional delivery strategies.

The conundrum is that there is no point for a debate on the film canon without companion professional support for film study. A look at existing well-regarded film study programs for elementary and secondary school educators can enlighten the development of a curriculum policy that supports formal film study within a specific school or district.

Formal Film Study Programs

To begin, we wish to distinguish between event-driven media programs and ongoing developmental cinema study. *Event-driven media programs* can stimulate interest and raise awareness for students. *Ongoing developmental cinema study* is thoughtful, scaffolded, long-term curriculum design akin to that of preK–12 language arts and literature. Both types are important; however, we should make film study part of an ongoing and planned program of study—rather than including event-driven experiences only.

The Academy of Motion Picture Arts and Sciences *Teacher's Guide Series*

The Academy of Motion Picture Arts and Sciences *Teacher's Guide Series* is an example of an event-driven program. This project took eight hundred students from the Los Angeles Public Schools on a three-day intensive site visit to the academy facility where they participated in screenings, observed panel discussions, and interacted with members of the film community. No doubt the program prompts interest and excitement about the nature of film and encourages film criticism, but as with all field-trip experiences, momentum is lost without integrated curriculum support.

The academy, in conjunction with the organization Young Minds Inspired, provides ten different study guides for teachers to help make the students' experience at the academy as impactful as possible. Each study guide has a letter to educators that introduces the guide and outlines the program's four objectives:

1. To enhance student interest in and knowledge about the motion picture development and production process

2. To encourage students to use critical thinking as they learn how filmmakers work

3. To engage students in an exploration of film as an art form and a medium to communication

4. To help students become more media literate

(Academy of Motion Pictures Arts and Sciences, n.d.)

There is free study guide for each of the following topics: animation, film editing, screenwriting, cinematography, art direction, media literacy, costumes and makeup, sound and music, documentaries, and visual effects. The topics include jobs in filmmaking (cinematography and film editing), genre (documentaries and animation), and skill set (media literacy). The website (www.oscars.org/education-outreach/teachersguide/index.html) is easy to access and navigate for the teacher wishing to consider an overview of each topic and look at specific student activities and their accompanying materials. The writing style used for the activities is discursive, rather than in a unit or lesson plan format, with a detailed background piece that includes a supplementary activity. In addition, there are four to five specific links to documents, images, and articles with short-question responses for students.

The Film Foundation Story of Movies Curriculum

Founded by Martin Scorsese in 1990, the Film Foundation is a nonprofit organization noted for its mission to preserve film and film history and to educate as well. The Story of Movies curriculum is coproduced with Turner Classic Movies and IBM. The board of directors is a veritable who's who of filmmakers, including George Lucas, Steven Spielberg, Ang Lee, Robert Redford, Woody Allen, and Peter Jackson.

The Story of Movies curriculum webpage (http://storyofmovies.org) features a video clip of directors Clint Eastwood and Martin Scorsese introducing the project. The site includes an active social professional learning network (in the Teacher's Lounge) with a place to connect with other users on a message board. As for the curriculum itself, the focus is primarily on middle school studies, with a well-developed unit of study on each of three film classics: *To Kill a Mockingbird*, *Mr. Smith Goes to Washington*, and *The Day the Earth Stood Still*. These selections may not connect with the contemporary learner's tastes, but they reflect the mission of the project: to support the traditions of the past and the rich history of cinema. This desire to inform students about their culture is not unlike the desire of an English teacher to introduce Mark Twain or Shakespeare or Jane Austen to the contemporary learner.

The program is organized around four focus chapters: (1) What Is a Movie?, (2) the Filmmaking Process, (3) Film Language and Elements of Style, and (4) Historical and Cultural Contexts. Within each chapter are sets of lesson plans including objectives, essential questions, scaffolded step-by-step activities, short drill tests with answer keys and formative assessment tasks, a glossary of key terms, and downloadable support materials. There are student activity booklets with response-to-screening sheets and worksheets. Of particular note is that the Story of Movies curriculum is aligned to a set of national film standards issued by the Film Foundation (Film Foundation, n.d.).

The U.K.'s Film Education Foundation

Espousing a strong long-term comprehensive policy cultivating film literacy across all classrooms, for twenty-five years, the Film Education Foundation of the United Kingdom directly connected to traditional reading and writing. Just as there has always been a concerted effort for students to use and enjoy words, the goal in their curriculum guidelines was to "help children and young people use, enjoy, and understand moving images. And not just to be technically capable, but to be culturally literate too" (Film Education Foundation, n.d.a).

The foundation supported a dynamic web presence and a long-term strategy to ensure that learners studied film dynamically. Unique, here, was a focus on professional development for all teachers at all levels. The foundation also provided free downloadable materials. The approach was under the guise of 21st century literature and organized film study for the primary years in sections on film in literacy, film trailers, and animation with a corresponding set of themes for secondary level students on film and English, citizenship, history, and film language.

For each level, there were specific film study materials for a range of quality films—many connected to books that have been adapted to film—with creative lesson plans and links. We particularly supported the Teaching Trailers page (www.filmeducation.org/teachingtrailers), which provided rich material for both elementary and secondary learners as they consider excerpting, essence grabbing, marketing, and sequencing a potent trailer. The foundation also supported an exciting event: the National Youth Film Festival (www.nationalyouthfilmfestival .org), which connects students with cinema.

As of the summer of 2013, the foundation is regrouping and hopes to take on a new format. What we admire is the approach, and we believe that like-minded film educators in other countries would do well to emulate the program. Visit www.thefilmspace.org for more information.

Five Instructional Tenets for Film Study in the Classroom

The examination of successful approaches to film study highlights the need for formal professional development regarding how to approach film study. This is particularly necessary since so few educators have had any formal training in cinema studies, let alone film production. Our hope and goal is for the formalized integration of film study and debate regarding a film canon in U.S. schools. We hope to see dynamic and engaging standards to guide school institutions in employing the best approaches possible to educate learners in what we see as a necessary literacy. Yet we know that, as always, it falls to teachers to make a difference. Our concern is that before professional teams dive into developing a canon of films for their local school, teachers need to have some teaching anchors to draw upon in order to design and deliver quality curriculum.

What are instructional tenets to assist teachers wishing to engage their students in film study? Drawing largely on Frank's extensive work in media literacy and film education instruction, we propose five tenets for film study instruction with accompanying resources to assist teachers who are ready to roll up their sleeves:

1. The languages of film
2. The critical role of screenwriting

3. The transition from passive to active viewer

4. A knowledge of the rules of filmmaking

5. The use of a popular film for the first experience

The Languages of Film

In 2006, Frank authored a film study guide to the 1962 Universal classic *To Kill a Mockingbird* (Baker, 2006). Film study guides traditionally help teachers understand how to go deeper when teaching a film so that their students better appreciate film literacy and film language. The goal of Frank's guide was to introduce the languages of film to U.S. literature teachers who were already using the film but might not have been teaching film literacy. It also introduces key vocabulary used in filmmaking (for example, *dissolve, cutaway, rule-of-thirds, montage, symbolism, juxtaposition,* and *deep focus*). He defines the *languages of film* as those tools and techniques used by filmmakers that assist in telling the story. The languages of film also help create meaning through:

- Cameras (lens, positioning, and movement)
- Lights
- Sound (including music and sound effects)
- Set design
- Postproduction (editing)
- Acting (including costumes, makeup, expressions, and body language)

As assuredly as a student learning to read needs to understand the meaning and power of terms such as *sentence, paragraph, metaphor,* and *analogy,* the same student needs to engage in understanding the key elements of media production. Cyrice Griffith-Siebens and Kim Alan Wheetley (2000) provide the following classic vocabulary and concepts critical to film study:

- Casting
- Cinematography
- Costume design
- Main title design
- Makeup and hairstyling
- Music
- Performing

- Picture editing

- Producing

- Production design and art direction

- Set decoration

- Sound effects

- Sound mixing

- Special visual effects

- Writing

Visit www.filmsite.org/filmterms2.html for additional terms in an illustrated guide to film terms.

The Critical Role of Screenwriting

Writing is of particular importance to film study. Given that we are communicating, persuading, and telling our cultural stories through film and video, we must raise the question, Why aren't we expecting and requiring our learners to write screenplays as part of their learning experiences? Media as writing is a rich entryway for teaching film. Teachers must encourage students to write first, before they ever pick up a camera and shoot an inch of video. Here is where we should teach them what a script looks like. (In film, it's called a *screenplay*.) Teaching students that screenplays contain only two elements, action and dialogue, often immediately engages students in revisiting their imagination and transferring their ideas to the page. It is a new way of writing for them and often a natural one.

A key experience is for both elementary and secondary students to have formal experiences examining a screenplay. Film studios publish screenplays as books, and starting with one of these might be useful. Magazines such as *Script* and *Creative Screenwriting* frequently include screenplay excerpts. Resources exist such as Simply Scripts and Script-O-Rama, an online compendium of available screenplays. Frank has a website devoted to scriptwriting in the classroom that provides educators with guidance and examples and books about the study of film that will support both teachers and students (www.frankwbaker.com).

The Transition From Passive to Active Viewer

Encouraging students to ask questions before, during, and after they watch is a key concept in both media and film education. Film Education (n.d.) recommends these questions:

- What is the purpose of the film, and how is it structured to suit this purpose?

- What devices are used to engage the audience?

- What do you think the central character is feeling at key points, and how has the filmmaker shown the audience their point of view?

- What is the setting, and why do you think the filmmaker chose it?

- What do you think is the message of the film, and how has it been communicated?

- How does the soundtrack affect your viewing of certain sequences in the film?

By asking these questions, our students become more acutely aware that films are designed to communicate a message. How that message is understood depends on how students interpret the way filmmakers tell a story using the tools at their disposal.

When most of us watch a film, we view passively, with the thinking parts of our brains switched off. We are usually relaxed and enjoying the movie. But in a classroom, that is not the posture we want our students to take. We want them to be active and critical viewers; we want them to be aware of how a certain technique might be used by the filmmaker to achieve certain goals and objectives. Filmmakers know and utilize specific rules and, for the most part, follow these rules when they create movies. We want educators and students to be cognizant of these rules when they watch. There is more to see than just an image on the screen; when watching film with a critical eye, we see other elements beyond just the image in the frame: we see lighting, expressions, set design, dialogue, music, and wardrobe. Film education makes the viewer aware of all the elements that make up the frame.

Film critic Roger Ebert (2008) suggests that films are best studied when we stop and pause the film and engage students in what he calls *shot-at-a-time analysis*. In fact, you don't have to own the film to pause and study the frame. The Internet Movie Database (IMDb) includes publicity stills from thousands of movies—a go-to site for students, film scholars, and filmmakers worldwide.

A Knowledge of the Rules of Filmmaking

There is a grammar to film. Films *can* be read—that is, analyzed, deconstructed, and interpreted. Not many of us have had sufficient training to feel comfortable teaching our students how to read a film, and it is not just film that has a grammar of sorts: video makers, television commercial producers, and game designers are all using some, if not all, of the same techniques and rules. *Reading film* means understanding and recognizing the tools, techniques, vocabulary, and rules of filmmaking.

Film director and producer George Lucas advocates teaching these rules: "Nobody (outside of art) teaches anybody about what screen direction is, what perspective is, what color is, what a diagonal line means. Those are rules; those are grammatical rules" (Edutopia, 2005). He goes on to say, "We also need to [help students] understand the importance of graphics, music, and cinema, which are just as powerful and in some ways more deeply intertwined with young people's culture" (Wikibooks, 2010). Elizabeth Daley, dean of the School of Cinematic Arts at the University of Southern California, agrees. She notes, "Such principles as screen direction, the placement of objects in the frame, color choices, morphing, cuts and dissolves all do much more than make a screen communication aesthetically pleasing. They are as critical to the creation of meaning as adverbs, adjectives, paragraphs, periods, analogies and metaphors are to text" (Daley, 2003).

For example, how you move the camera and how you position the camera have meaning. When camera angles look up to a character (shooting up), they make him or her appear more important and prominent; looking down at a character (shooting down) makes the character appear small and powerless.

There are also rules in lighting, costuming, set design, music, and sound. After a film has been shot, it goes into postproduction, where more rules are put into practice. Films communicate in many ways, and trained teachers have many opportunities to enlighten their students in the following areas:

- Special effects
- Color
- Lighting
- Symbolism
- Music
- Set design

There are rules in editing as well as in shooting that are critical to the study of film. Filmmakers must craft a story to engage the audience and then edit the film in a compelling and fluid format. We will use the example of James Cameron's film *Titanic*. Most people are already familiar with the story of the "unsinkable" cruise ship that struck an iceberg on its maiden voyage in 1912, sinking in the frozen Atlantic Ocean waters, killing more than 1,500 people. In a very real sense, Cameron had a plot problem because his audience knew the ending in advance. In *Titanic*, the screenwriter wraps the story of the ill-fated voyage around the fictional love story between a stowaway, Jack (played by actor Leonardo DiCaprio), and a wealthy woman about to be married, Rose (portrayed by actress Kate Winslet). Much of story is told in a *flashback*, a cinematic device in which we go back in time. As the film moves back and forth from present to past, it uses the editing technique of *dissolve* where one image slowly fades away, while another appears. As the film begins, we meet Rose as an older woman, one of the last survivors. The film also flashes forward as she reminisces, in present day, about the ship and her relationship with Jack on the ill-fated voyage.

Many middle school students believe this is a true story, and one of the reasons might be the director's use of the dissolve. The use of a dissolve usually indicates a passage in time. It can also mean a change in location. Director Cameron shows Jack and Rose embracing on the bow of the *Titanic*, then the image dissolves (slowly one picture fades away while another picture appears), and the audience sees the real *Titanic* with actual footage shot with underwater cameras. By dissolving from fictional ship to the real one, Cameron is taking the audience into the story *and* making us believe that what we are seeing is real. (To see the dissolve sequence in *Titanic*, visit www.frankwbaker.com/titanic.htm.)

The Use of a Popular Film for the First Experience

One approach to film studies is to first use a popular, mainstream film with your students. Students will already be familiar with the film's characters, actors, and plot, which will allow you to go deeper into the filmmaker's rules and techniques. For example, a teacher might choose to show the Disney Pixar film *WALL-E*. A key reason for using this film with young people is that they likely know the plot: a lone robot remains on a future Earth to clean up the mess by compacting trash, while humans have been relegated to a couch-potato lifestyle aboard a cruise-like spaceship, with a promise of return once Earth is clean again. The reason this is a particularly potent choice is that the opening eight minutes contain virtually no dialogue, so viewers must pay attention in order to follow the action.

The strategy here is to have participants view these eight minutes *without any background or instruction*. Please note that this works well even if the students have never seen the film. The premise is that viewers tend to pay attention to the opening of any film and actively pick up clues strategically placed there by the director. *WALL-E* is no different.

In this activity, after the first screening, the teacher distributes fifteen index cards, each with a different instruction. Participants read the card, or share it if they're working in groups, and then pay careful attention as the opening scene is screened a second time. After the second screening, participants read their card aloud and answer the questions posed.

For older students, another option is to screen the opening eight minutes of Steven Spielberg's film *E.T. the Extra-Terrestrial*. Like *WALL-E*, the beginning of the film has virtually no dialogue, just action, so paying attention is important. The opening scene of E.T.'s discovery and abandonment by the alien spaceship uses many film techniques. Applying the same strategy, first watch the film with no instruction, distribute some film questions on index cards, watch again, and discuss.

Once students have experience and are comfortable with understanding the languages of film, the critical role of screenwriting, the need for active film viewing, an examination of the rules of filmmaking, and a guided introduction to an accessible application to a popular film, they will have a deeper appreciation and more fulfilling film-viewing experience.

Capturing and Cultivating Student Cinema Interest

In addition to formal film study, schools can support student interest in film studies and generate an interest in films and filmmaking with extracurricular opportunities. School faculties and individual teachers can sponsor a film club in which students come together on a regular basis to further their fascination with motion pictures in the same spirit as book clubs or chess club. There are no set criteria for what a film club does, but the United Kingdom has a model that has flourished. Its website, FilmClub (www.filmclub.org), describes the benefits to participating schools:

- Free training to give teachers and schools ideas and help in setting up and running their own club

- A free license allowing teachers to watch films in the classroom (as part of the club and during lesson times)

- Free DVDs sent to the school, which are then simply sent back after viewing

- Access to an interactive website where staff and students can find out about films, add ratings, write reviews, and add films to their wish lists

- The possibility of visits from members of the film industry

- Funding to support film clubs when they are up and running successfully

Starting such a club is relatively easy; when an educator announces plans to form a film club, students usually show up, though the screening of a timely and engaging film tends to generate interest quickly. Club members should not only screen films (on high-quality high-definition television screens with digital sound capabilities, if possible) but also focus on dissecting scenes by concentrating on the languages of film noted earlier in this chapter. Students collaboratively decide which film genres to prioritize for their viewing and begin to understand conventions common to the genre of narrative, documentary, shorts, and animation.

Film clubs often provide cameras, lights, sound equipment, and more to young people for the purpose of having them create and edit films and film trailers. Students can learn the scriptwriting and storyboarding processes—critical steps prior to filming. Educators already know that when they put cameras into the hands of their students, they empower them to tell stories that are meaningful and that they will want to share with others. It is no wonder that Animoto, YouTube, Vimeo, and other sharing sites are flourishing.

If the club has a website, blog, or e-newsletter, students may want to write and post reviews. Having students read a film critic's regular reviews and write their own supports critical standards for being responsive and responsible thinkers. What is more, reviews are important to audiences and for box office sales. The business side of the film industry can be a fascinating area for students to study. This includes creating the seed idea for a film, pitching the idea to raise the funding, filming on the set, editing, moving onto postproduction, screening at a major festival, and working to find a distributor who then negotiates with theater owners. Teachers can arrange visits from local filmmakers or connect with them via Skype. When students have the opportunities to question filmmakers, they invariably begin to understand and appreciate the skills and careers involved in movie making.

Ultimately, we support the creation of an annual film festival in a school under the cosponsorship of the film club, English department, and visual and media arts department, with a set of four to six films shown along with student-made productions for the school and larger community. A film festival gives purpose and heft to the film club with a dynamic event to create a vital community of informed filmgoers.

A film club is a potentially marvelous extracurricular experience, but the primary focus of this chapter is the lack of formal attention to film study that occurs within the school curriculum. The most formal way to give film study the attention it deserves is through the creation of a schoolwide film canon.

Creating a Schoolwide Film Canon

Curriculum is choice making. There is no Athena, the Greek goddess of wisdom, sitting on our school boards to assist with what is truly one of the great responsibilities of educators. What content, skills, assessments, and ideas are deemed most critical for a specific group of learners? Do we employ standards as proficiency targets? On the most concrete level, what historical periods do we include? Which do we leave out? What works of art and music do we emphasize? Which approach to the teaching do we embrace? Which scientific theories from the past and which new breakthroughs do we examine? What works of literature will be foundational and required? Obviously there are no right and wrong answers, but there are often common trends and habits that emerge on book lists for learners. Above all, there is always the pervasive issue of *taste*, which is unique and individual. The reality is that a group of educators or a group of community members will share their taste, their personal experience, and negotiate with each other to make choices.

We advocate wrestling with a film canon because it seems a reasonable way to break the pattern of curriculum neglect. Let us consider what might be possible criteria for making curriculum decisions on great film works for our learners to examine. We wish to reinforce that unlike literature, film is a different medium with images in motion, actors, sets, angles, and sound to be considered in addition to the very story or information being shared. Let us explore the criteria established by a member of the film community, a national approach, and a school's approach to determine a method for finding criteria.

The widely regarded writer and director Paul Schrader (2006) wrote a touchstone article titled *Canon Fodder* in which he suggests six criteria to determine a great film:

1. **Beauty**—Relating to how the aesthetics change our perception of reality

2. **Strangeness**—Reflecting originality and the unpredictable

3. **Uniformity of form and content**—Seamlessly integrating the format and presentation of the film with the subject matter

4. **Tradition**—Demonstrating a relationship to prior works of art

5. **Repeatability**—Showing that the work stands up over time

6. **Viewer engagement**—Promoting active viewer emotional and intellectual involvement

What is appealing about Schrader's criteria is that he emphasizes those qualities and traits that should be considered, rather than simply listing his canon-worthy choices. By contrast, Canada has taken a national approach to the development of a film canon.

Canada's National Approach

With its unique and consistent commitment, the government of Canada has supported the cultivation of its own filmmaking and film-viewing community since 1939 with the passage of the National Film Act, which led to the National Film Board (NFB) of Canada. For over seventy years, Canada has formally supported filmmaking and viewing. Its dynamic and exciting website, the National Film Board of Canada Education (www.nfb.ca/education), provides thoughtful education resources, teaching guides, and an abundance of resources. Most telling is its approach to a canon of Canadian-produced films. Its list of over two thousand films is a broad, wide-ranging "mega-canon." Educators have direct support for inspiring young people interested in expressing their ideas and stories through film and, by equal measure, a desire to have a film-literate population. What is noteworthy, though, in the listing is a short section of newly released films each year that have been featured as "winners" through a jury process. Indeed, juries or panels are a mainstay of film festivals, where each year a select group considers submissions. This model can readily be replicated in an individual school wishing to support the development of a film canon.

The Festival Jury Model

The criteria for filmmakers submitting films to three of the most prominent film festivals—Sundance, TIFF (Toronto International Film Festival), and Cannes—are primarily technical. The juries first want to ensure that each film matches specifications in a category, such as narrative, short subject, animation, and full-length documentary. Acceptance into the festival is actually acceptance to a canon for that particular year. Prizes appear to be awarded by the value set for each unique jury. It is here that perhaps we might find some grounding for criteria for a film-canon menu for teachers to choose from with periodic additions of new releases through a jury model.

Film Canon Model

We propose a model for building a film canon that draws from many of the programs we have referenced in this chapter. We propose that schools compile a large bank of vetted movies that meet criteria, as with the National Film Board of Canada, the Film Education Foundation of the United Kingdom, the Academy of Motion Picture Arts and Sciences *Teacher's Guide Series*, and the Film Foundation's Story of Movies project. Films in the canon should:

- Match the interests and readiness of the age group
- Provide insight into the human condition
- Engage the student audience
- Integrate with curriculum study within or across subject areas
- Represent a specific genre—narrative, documentary, short, animation, and so on

- Employ a range of filmmaking techniques that support the story or information
- Have a flow of story or ideas that is natural and paced effectively
- Demonstrate the unique possibilities of film versus other media
- Capture the viewer through cinematography and angles
- Use compelling and engaging editing

Conclusion: The Film Canon Project K–12

The formal and deliberate study of a film canon should be a pillar in the contemporary K–12 curriculum. To address the basic premise articulated in this chapter that we need this formal film study and a film canon in our schools, we have created the Film Canon Project for grades K–12 (http://filmcanonproject .org), an open and free arena to propose and post films for teachers to use in their classrooms. Our sincere hope is that a teacher seeking to expand and concurrently deepen student film viewing will find the site a genuine help. Whether seeking to support a science curriculum unit with a documentary or to investigate the human condition through a classic narrative film, teachers can search the site to find resources. The films in the canon are organized by elementary, middle, and high school levels. Each film is tagged with the director, rating, production release year, a synopsis, and the link to IMDb. More importantly, we encourage readers of this book and students to submit additional titles for consideration and inclusion. Figure 4.1 shows a screen capture from the website.

Figure 4.1: The Film Canon Project.

The project encourages dynamic and engaged discussion regarding film, and it serves as a clearinghouse of film study resources that is continually updated. A virtual jury (including students) is a particularly important feature of the project. Schools can use this resource to then select their own canon. This determination of appropriate films combined with film literacy standards provides a basis for an exciting and stimulating curriculum design to inspire 21st century learners.

References and Resources

Academy of Motion Picture Arts and Sciences. (n.d.). *Teacher's guide series.* Accessed at www.oscars.org/education-outreach/teachersguide/index.html on October 23, 2012.

Baker, F. (2006). *Film study guide for* To Kill a Mockingbird*: Seeing the film through the lens of media literacy.* Accessed at www.frankwbaker.com/tkam.htm on May 12, 2013.

Bowers, J. M. (n.d.). *Western literary canon in context* [Online course]. Accessed at www.thegreatcourses.com/tgc/courses/course_detail.aspx?cid=2120 on May 9, 2013.

British Film Institute. (2012). *Film: 21st century literacy strategy—A report for the use of film education in ITT and CPD within UK teaching schools and universities.* Accessed at www.21stcenturyliteracy.org.uk/docs/Film%20Ed%20in%20ITT%20&%20 CPD%20Report_FINAL.pdf on October 23, 2012.

Daley, E. (2003). Expanding the concept of literacy. *EDUCAUSE Review, 38*(2), 33–40. Accessed at http://net.educause.edu/ir/library/pdf/erm0322.pdf on May 12, 2013.

Ebert, R. (2008, August 30). *How to read a movie* [Web log post]. Accessed at www.rogerebert.com/rogers-journal/how-to-read-a-movie on May 12, 2013.

Edutopia. (2005, June 1). *George Lucas: Teaching "communication"* [Video file]. Accessed at www.edutopia.org/george-lucas-teaching-communication-video on October 23, 2012.

Film Education. (n.d.a). *Black history month: Interrogating film texts.* Accessed at www .filmeducation.org/resources/secondary/topics/black_history_month/interrogating _film_texts on October 23, 2012.

Film Education. (n.d.b). *Film in the classroom: Introduction.* Accessed at www.filmeducation.org/staffroom/film_in_the_classroom/21st_century_literacy on May 12, 2013.

Film Foundation. (n.d.). *National Film Study Standards for middle school.* Accessed at www.storyofmovies.org/common/11041/PDFs/NationalFilmStudyStandards.pdf on May 12, 2013.

Griffith-Siebens, C., & Wheetley, K. A. (2000). *A framework for teaching & learning through the arts & technologies of television.* Los Angeles, CA: Academy of

Television Arts and Sciences Foundation. Accessed at www.emmys.tv/sites /emmys.tv/files/framework.pdf on May 12, 2013.

IMDb. (2002, February 22). *E.T. the Extra-Terrestrial (1982)*. Accessed at www.imdb.com/media/rm3028916480/tt0083866 on June 4, 2013.

Jacobs, H. H. (2012). *Mapping to the core: Integrating the Common Core standards into our local school curriculum*. Midvale, UT: School Improvement Network.

Landow, G. P. (1989). *The literary canon*. Accessed at www.victorianweb.org/gender /canon/litcan.html on October 23, 2012.

Le Voyage dans la lune. (n.d.). In Wikipedia. Accessed at http://en.wikipedia.org/wiki /File:Le_Voyage_dans_la_lune.jpg#filelinks on June 3, 2013.

Schrader, P. (2006). Canon fodder: As the sun finally sets on the century of cinema, by what criteria do we determine its masterworks? *Film Comment*, 33–49. Accessed at http://paulschrader.org/articles/pdf/2006-FilmComment_Schrader .pdf on October 24, 2012.

Wikibooks. (2010). *Technology integration in K12 education/digital storytelling in social studies*. Accessed at http://en.wikibooks.org/wiki/Technology_Integration_In _K12_Education/Digital_Storytelling_in_Social_Studies on October 23, 2012.

Young, C. A., Long, S., & Myers, J. (2010). Editorial: Enhancing English language arts education with digital video. *Contemporary Issues in Technology and Teacher Education*, *10*(1), 7–19. Accessed at www.editlib.org/p/34121 on November 8, 2013.

Mark Schulte, MA, directs education outreach for the Pulitzer Center on Crisis Reporting. He uses the journalism supported by the Pulitzer Center to engage students on under-reported global topics such as water and sanitation, extractives and commodities, climate change, women and children in crisis, and food insecurity. The education program at the Pulitzer Center, called Global Gateway, reached more than 10,000 students in the United States and Europe in 2012.

Prior to his work at the Pulitzer Center, Mark taught global issues–based journalism for nearly ten years. Earlier he worked as a magazine writer and editor, covering politics and education in Virginia, and ultimately converted the magazine into a web journal of college life.

A confirmed tech enthusiast, Mark is interested in using innovative tools to connect students globally to their world and to each other. At a time of considerable superficiality and silliness online, he believes students should be encouraged to create a positive digital footprint of meaningful work.

Mark graduated from Oberlin College and holds a master's degree in interactive journalism from American University.

To learn more about Mark's work, visit www.markschulte.com.

Jennie L. Johnson, MEd, is an experienced teacher and educational consultant who has filled a myriad of roles. She has worked as a curriculum and technology coordinator in Des Moines Public Schools; a curriculum, assessment, and data specialist and K–12 language arts department chair in Ankeny Community School District; a high school English teacher in districts in Iowa and Minnesota; and a national consultant in Mapping to the Core, assessment, and data analysis.

Jennie has also led groups of K–12 teachers and administrators in creating a district assessment system that included performance assessment and standards-based reporting instruments. In addition, she has assisted teachers in revising their consensus maps aligned to the Common Core in the state of Alaska, in Kansas City, and in Chicago area schools.

Jennie has presented at conferences on Mapping to the Core, coauthored a chapter in *Getting Results With Curriculum Mapping*, and was featured in the *Video Journal of Education*'s series, *Integrating Literacy Instruction Across the Curriculum*. In conjunction with the Pulitzer Center, she has developed consensus unit maps that teachers can access from the Pulitzer website. She has a bachelor's degree in English and a master's degree in curriculum and instruction.

To book Mark or Jennie for professional development, contact pd@solution-tree.com.

Chapter 5
Examining New Media Journalism: Global Perspectives and Possibilities

By Mark Schulte and Jennie L. Johnson

News itself is new today. The manner in which most Americans obtain their information has been transformed by the Internet. It is fast-paced, with accelerated delivery systems creating a news cycle measured in minutes or even seconds, rather than by days. It is atomized, with a virtual cacophony of voices speaking with wildly varying levels of information and authority. It is mobile, reaching people in the most unlikely places at every moment of the day on their laptops and cell phones. It is opinion driven, with analysis, slant, and bias occupying ever more bandwidth. And it is radically democratized, allowing a student tapping away in her bedroom the same potential audience as a decorated journalist at a prominent professional news organization.

This readily available news and instant gratification for what is happening in the world is quite different as journalism has been struggling with the changing media scene and engagement of audiences with global news and issues.

Many traditional journalists did not think to engage actively with their audiences. They often wrote more for their editors and the subjects of their articles than for the actual readers of the work. Many journalists neglected to think about how and why, or whether the stories were relevant to the majority of their readers' lives. Also, these same journalists often did not think about how to obtain and sustain engagement in the issues addressed in their articles, except for the editorial pages or longer and continued investigative journalism articles. Not only was the subject of engagement overlooked by journalists, but also very little thought was given to collaboration across media platforms. The competition among journalists and owners of newspapers kept them from reaching out to other compatriots across the country and around the world to produce articles that complemented and added to the conversation.

In the past, journalists would travel to a location where something of global importance was occurring, such as the floods in Iowa in 1993. While in Iowa, the journalists would interview witnesses and survivors and write a story with some photographs or video. Several major stories could be filed in a few days, and then, the journalist returned home. If any follow-up to the story was published or covered on television, it would be smaller pieces about Des Moines and central Iowa being without water for ten days, but there was no cooperation among affiliates and no continued interaction with listeners, readers, or viewers.

Today, journalists, editors, and news media outlets are more open to multi-platform, cross-media collaboration in ways they would never have dreamed of before. Now, journalists can access news and sources immediately through their Internet and social media connections to people and sources around the world. Information, video, sounds, and music can be transported across the globe from one journalist to another. Journalists can build on information obtained from other journalists and the general public. After breaking the first story, journalists can follow up on the story and show the public how the news is unfolding with a constant stream of information from around the world that is readily available and not protected by one single journalist or newspaper. In addition, the collection and analysis of comments from various media sources allow readers, listeners, and viewers the opportunity to ask questions or suggest other angles to the story that journalists might then investigate and produce. Follow-up stories are now prompted by emotions and feelings that will increase the compassion that global citizens have for each other. The journalist now has access to multiple perspectives and views that he or she can pursue for additional stories.

The media not only reports news today; it can also create news like Twitter did during the Arab Spring. The impact and importance of the role that social media played in the demonstrations and uprisings of the Arab Spring have been debated in depth with supporters on both sides of the issue: social media was the instigator of the demonstrations, or social media was only a tool in providing information about the uprisings. Whichever view a person supports, one thing is certain: the perception of social media and its importance to the communication of global news has definitely changed. Through Twitter, Facebook, and other social media sites, the world was able to stay abreast of what was happening in Egypt, Syria, and other Arab countries, and organizers of uprisings communicated with their demonstrators and refined plans for trying to wrest the power away from current rulers. The information on display for the world to ingest came in various forms of media, such as images, music, art, and video. These media not only showed what was happening in Arab nations but also depicted some of the history of those Arab nations and predicted what changes might occur and the impact the changes might have on the Arab people and the population of the world. The Arab Spring and the media absolutely demonstrated the influence and power of social media in its ability to keep the world abreast of global news and to organize group actions across the globe. Today, journalists, editors, and news media outlets are open to multiplatform, cross-media collaboration in ways they would never have dreamed of before.

Journalism's Global Literacy Focus

One major example of a global focus in journalism is the Pulitzer Center on Crisis Reporting. The center was formed in 2006 out of a conversation between Jon Sawyer, longtime Washington bureau chief for the *St. Louis Post-Dispatch*, and that paper's owner, Emily Rauh Pulitzer. In the midst of a major contraction in the journalism industry, Sawyer and Pulitzer saw an opportunity to create a new model of support for global news coverage, one that sought to learn from the mistakes of the earlier models and seize new opportunities.

The Pulitzer Center's approach is to support global literacy by identifying and funding journalism projects on important global problems that, while widespread and rooted in long-term historical trends, are under-reported in the media.

Since the mid-1990s, when web browsers such as Netscape and wildly popular online services such as America Online brought a tsunami of free information into the homes of millions of Americans, the budgets of virtually every large journalism institution have been slashed. Foreign correspondence, always the least-read and most expensive piece of any given news organization, was first on the chopping block. As the journalism industry struggled to adjust to a changing media market that expected its news free and online, and a business model that was upended by web services such as Craigslist (which rendered want ads obsolete), international bureaus closed, foreign correspondents were laid off, and serious global stories went uncovered. This contraction has only worsened over the years, and while some promising and exciting new private models have emerged in this try-anything period of journalistic change, no financially sustainable solution has been found so far, and a generation is growing up amid a dearth of good global news.

Further, the global news stories that do find their way into the pages and broadcasts of the companies that have survived have tended toward an instant-gratification narrative that seeks out the tragedy of the moment, depicts it along familiar lines, and leaves the story aside quickly in favor of the next bomb blast or natural disaster. Yet, there are reams of stories to be told that reveal a world more connected, more mutually dependent, than ever. Stories that look beyond the shock of the moment—a suicide bombing in Kabul, a famine in Eritrea, a pirate attack off the coast of Yemen—to identify the root causes of these problems, to shed light on the humans who experience them, and to help the reader make sense of a world that is more than just the sum of a series of sensational events.

The Pulitzer Center seeks out projects that attempt to do just that and increase media and global literacy in its readers and users. Each project covers a specific topic: gold mining in the Peruvian rain forest, clean water access in resource-rich Nigeria, or child marriage in Afghanistan. These projects are grouped into broader topics called Gateways on the Pulitzer Center's website (http://pulitzercenter.org /gateways). Three examples of these Gateways include Downstream, a collection of projects, articles, and information that addresses the global water and sanitation crisis, which affects billions and will continue to cause even more serious problems for future generations; Global Goods, Local Costs, which examines the often overlooked human and environmental costs that accompany resource extraction; and Food Insecurity, which looks at the destabilizing effects of mass hunger worldwide. These problems and crises have affected many of the world's citizens and have been chronicled by a myriad of journalists on the Pulitzer Center's website. The Gateways section of the website reports on these global problems using a variety of media.

This Pulitzer Center model has taken off like wildfire, owing in part to the savvy with which Sawyer and his small team have used their resources and in part to the totality of the collapse of commercial journalism, which has led to an impressive response among the foundations that support the Pulitzer Center's work. With over three hundred completed projects and some eighty-five under-way as of this writing, the Pulitzer Center has proven that its innovative model can make major contributions to media and global literacy with surprisingly modest funding. Major media outlets including *The New York Times, PBS NewsHour, The Atlantic, Foreign Policy*, and *National Geographic* have published the work of Pulitzer Center journalists. Their commitment to using new forms and blending media in creative ways has garnered both an Emmy and a Webby award for their online work.

Historically, journalists have tended to work in one medium or another without blending the two or crossing over. Some are writers, some photographers, and some videographers, but their employers typically did not encourage them to use more than one medium in their reporting. Similarly, journalism projects themselves tended to blend media only in established ways. For example, a print article might carry with it several straightforward photographs depicting some important elements of the article, or a video might use some explanatory text, and so forth.

The Pulitzer Center has encouraged its grantees to expand their skill sets in supporting and encouraging media literacy by asking photographers to write, writers to take photographs, and both to use video in creative ways for blog posts and Meet the Journalist sessions. This action has led to some startlingly effective pieces, including an audio slideshow created by writer Anna Badkhen (2011) that brought to life a Ramadan ice cream break enjoyed by children who lived near where she was staying in Mazar-e-Sharif, in northern Afghanistan. Badkhen, normally a writer only, took photographs and wrote and recorded the script for the piece. With images narrated in Badkhen's distinctive Russian accent, the slideshow presents a side of life in the war-torn country that would not have been possible to convey in the same way in print.

The viewer and reader of Badkhen's work follows along as a story of the intense heat of the July Ramadan in the area, when "mercury climbed to 120 degrees and stayed there for a week," gives way to an evening van ride to patronize some street ice cream vendors, finishing as the mothers "filed behind a curtain that separated women from men so they could enjoy their Ramadan treat in segregated peace" (Badkhen, 2011).

The pictures of the ice cream break and the narration of the children's stories about growing up in the midst of war helped students around the world identify with these photographic images of children who were just like them, but whose lives were very different because of the political strife in their country. Students could identify with the brief escape from the reality of their lives that these Arab children experienced through something as simple as an ice cream break.

Another example of this innovative media blending can be found in a project called *Voices From Haiti*. Renowned poet Kwame Dawes, himself of Caribbean heritage, wrote a series of poems inspired by photographs taken by Pulitzer Center grantee Andre Lambertson, who took more than a dozen trips to Haiti following the devastating 2011 earthquake that killed hundreds of thousands and left an already-impoverished nation with yet more heartbreak. Lambertson's photographs, which depicted the lives of ordinary Haitians persevering in the face of crippling poverty, disease, and displacement, inspired Dawes to compose moving portraits in poetry, which he recorded in English and Haitian Creole, over a slideshow of the photographs set to a spare and haunting musical score.

In "Mother of Mothers," one of the poems in the *Voices From Haiti* collection, Dawes (n.d.) has written a paean to the women of the island. "You must draw the line of defense around the beleaguered souls," he says, as Lambertson's images of multiple generations of Haitian women, some in hospitals, some at prayer, some at home, flicker by. The piece deftly and movingly draws the listener away from a view of Haiti that might be defined by violence or aggression, presenting in images, music, and the rich tones of Dawes's voice a powerful testament to the collective strength of generations of its women (Pulitzer Center on Crisis Reporting, January 2011).

The blended pictures, music, and poetry provide motivation in the form of models that readers, viewers, and listeners can imitate to persevere in not only the aftermath of the catastrophe in Haiti but also other hardships in life.

This project, which pushes the boundaries of what has traditionally been considered journalism, is available at http://pulitzercenter.org/features/voices-haiti and has taken life in performances at a theater festival in New York City, a university of Miami event, and in Port-au-Prince itself. Together, the poems, photographs, and music reach the viewer in a way that a traditional written article, however masterfully composed, simply could not.

Resources for Educational Institutions

The Pulitzer Center treats the projects it commissions, which typically comprise one or two major articles or videos, three blog posts, and a Meet the Journalist video, not as single pieces of reporting to be published and then left aside as archives but rather as sustained campaigns that spark discussions and interactions that continue long after the story is published. A critical component of this is the educational outreach that is done in secondary schools, colleges, and universities.

With active programs in St. Louis, Chicago, Washington, DC, Philadelphia, and Europe, and free online materials available to anyone with an Internet connection, the Pulitzer Center's education program, called Global Gateway, has become a deep resource for thousands of students and their teachers.

The Pulitzer Center works with students in a variety of age groups in rural and urban communities. Some are well-traveled global citizens already, and some have never left their neighborhoods. Pulitzer Center education specialists are flexible in how they interact with students, tailoring the engagement to suit the needs of the class. Also, Pulitzer Center journalists focus on global literacy to bring personal narratives to large, faceless issues that many U.S. students struggle to comprehend.

Consider how much more compelling it is for a student to learn about the impact of the earthquake in Haiti by looking at photographs of a family taken over a period of months and hearing their stories from a journalist who lived among the survivors of the Haitian earthquake or a writer who was embedded with another family in Mazar-e-Sharif, Afghanistan, far from the front lines of the war, where most journalists spend their time. Recognizing and gaining greater understanding of systemic issues that impact local communities is one of the most significant challenges young people today face. But problems that span the globe and affect millions of people can be difficult to connect meaningfully to the lives of students precisely because of their scale. How does one put a face on water and sanitation, on food security, on the extraction of commodities that make up the products he or she uses every day? Yet, these are precisely the issues that affect one's environment, health, security, economy, and community.

This is especially true when students exist in an environment—their school, neighborhood, or online social circle—that does not include a regular diet of good global journalism. Students today face an information paradox. Their news frequently comes from friends' recommendations, tweets, and emails. It is often unverified and presented without context. The Internet, especially the social web, has made information more available than it has ever been before, but this torrent of often poorly documented data can be overwhelming at best, alienating at worst. And even with good information, how can society move beyond a model that locks young people into the role of information consumers? The best learning happens when students are active contributors to the process, what some educators call "owning" the learning. What might this look like in the context of global journalism?

In Chicago, the Pulitzer Center has for several years partnered with a youth media organization to bring the previously mentioned issues to life. Free Spirit Media, a cutting-edge video production group that is active in schools throughout the city's underserved south and west sides, offers classes that teach young people the grammar and syntax of good filmmaking. In their programs, students learn how to create a quality product with correct lighting and sound, a good mix of shots, and an effective tempo.

Pulitzer Center journalists work with Free Spirit Media instructors and the students to provide overviews of broad topics such as maternal health, food security, or water and make them accessible through the journalism and mentorship of the reporters and finally to provide guidance as the students create their own documentaries on local subjects that are informed by the global topics at hand. The results of this partnership have been gratifying. Over the years, student teams in Chicago have made several dozen films on subjects of their own choosing—but always with a connection to a larger global issue.

One such team of girls who made a short documentary on the sometimes-hidden subject of lesbian, gay, bisexual, and transgender (LGBT) students in their schools and communities won a student prize in the Media That Matters film festival, an event that recognizes short-form social-issue media (Free Spirit Media, 2010). The girls, who have never left their home city, and who were significantly outside of their comfort zones in reporting on LGBT issues, were prompted by Pulitzer Center journalists to seek out stories that connected to the Pulitzer Center Gateway titled Women, Children, Crisis. This Gateway seeks to illuminate the adversity and outright crimes visited upon women and children disproportionately worldwide. The discrimination faced by LGBT teens at home and in the community is a good example of how global problems show up in local neighborhoods (Pulitzer Center on Crisis Reporting, 2009).

Other students have made films on water pollution in Lake Michigan, undocumented immigrant teens, and sexually transmitted diseases in youth populations. All of these are topics chosen by the students, with interviews and footage obtained by them in their communities but with intimate connections to broad global challenges introduced by Pulitzer Center journalists.

Teachers and students can access written articles by prominent journalists to use in projects and as models for writing to improve their media literacy. In addition, they can view videos, listen to music, and participate in blogs about topics included in the Gateways to use in classroom projects and increase their knowledge and use of media literacy. Students and teachers can also connect with other students, teachers, and classrooms from around the world who are concerned about similar global issues. The classrooms could work on projects together so that all students can recognize different perspectives that arise out of working with others who live in different circumstances. These opportunities would improve and reinforce the global literacy of students.

A Journalistic Walk Around the World

In January 2013, two-time Pulitzer Prize–winning journalist Paul Salopek began a walk around the world, following in the footsteps of our common ancestors out of the Great Rift Valley of Africa all the way to Patagonia, the tip of the last continent to be discovered some 12,000 years ago. This remarkable project is called Out of Eden, a title that hints at the walk's mission: to retrace the path of human migration at foot level, walking three miles per hour, through the untold stories of our present day.

The walk will take seven years and will draw on Salopek's wealth of experience as a conflict journalist who has covered more than sixty countries, including some twenty wars, in his decorated career as a foreign correspondent. The articles he writes along the trail, in a style he calls *slow journalism*, will be published in *National Geographic* magazine. In the face of what he calls a "tsunami of nano-headlines generated by the digital age," which render many of us paralyzed by information overload and unable to see the bigger global picture, Salopek will be seeking out the overlooked narratives that tie all humans together. He believes his walking pace will allow him to observe people, places, and trends that most journalists—indeed, most people—overlook because they are moving too fast in today's technology-laden world.

It is a project that encompasses many of the themes that the Pulitzer Center's journalism seeks to address, including migration and human displacement, the roots of conflict, the effects of climate change on mass populations and ecosystems, and the unforeseen consequences of foreign aid on fragile cultures. What makes this project different, apart from its vast scope, is its technique. Most international correspondents fly or drive into big stories when they happen—a civil war breaks out, a natural disaster hits, a bomb goes off in a marketplace—and leave as soon as their stories are filed, often just days after arriving. Much is missed, much overlooked. By walking into stories, wearing clothes picked up at local souks and carrying less than thirty pounds of gear on his back, Salopek believes he will be able to find the untold global stories that escape the notice of the so-called *parachute journalists*.

The trek will also allow him to tie stories together in ways that are rarely done, providing a narrative that emphasizes connections between people and places—stories from the roads that lead increasing numbers of people to the world's megacities, rather than accounts only from the cities themselves—and will, at its end, provide a unifying view of what it was like to live on many overlooked parts of planet Earth during those seven years.

Most exciting from an educational perspective, the walk presents a remarkable opportunity for teachers and students to follow along. Far from being a hermetic retreat from civilization, the walk will invite learners to interact with Salopek consistently through video chats, question-and-answer sessions, Twitter, and other methods of digital conversation. These interactions will take place through the *Walk to Learn* blog, a community of learners cultivated by Project Zero (http://walktolearn.outofedenwalk.com) and the Pulitzer Center's project page for the Out of Eden walk (http://pulitzercenter.org/projects/out-of-eden).

With a satellite phone and an ultra-light laptop, Salopek will be in constant communication with teams at the Pulitzer Center, Project Zero, *National Geographic*, and others. The world's proliferation of Internet cafes will allow him to connect via Skype and Google Hangouts, sharing his observations with students, answering their questions, and following up on their suggestions to investigate stories that connect to themes they are studying. This journalistic walk around the world will provide students with an opportunity to interact with Salopek, suggesting places he might investigate, ethnic groups he might seek out and interview, and routes he might take. It is an unprecedented opportunity for students of all ages throughout the world.

"Let me be your foreign correspondent," he told thousands of middle and high school students in the Pulitzer Center's education network during a speaking tour of Chicago, St. Louis, Washington, DC, and Philadelphia public and independent schools just two months before his departure (Salopek, 2012). *National Geographic* and the Knight Foundation (2012) are funding the Out of Eden walk's fieldwork and journalism. The walk's educational mission is supported by the Pulitzer Center on Crisis Reporting and Project Zero, an educational research group at the Harvard Graduate School of Education. Visit www.outofedenwalk .com to find out more about the walk, including maps of the route traveled so far, and a rough outline of the total trip.

Accessing and Using Social and New Media

For far too long, professional journalism has existed as a simple one-time information transfer from reporter to reader. The explosion of the social web, which has seen the rise of social networking and blogging services like Facebook, Tumblr, and Twitter, has changed the way the people who find their information on the Internet think about their role as media consumers. Today, the comments section of a piece of online media can be as important as the media itself, and the debates sparked there often take on lives of their own, lasting weeks or months. The conversation and interaction among individuals based on news and information has become as important as the original content.

Online journalism is no different, though many journalists have perhaps been slow to accept it. In part, this is a legacy problem arising from the assumption on the part of the news industry that the media consumer's role is merely to consume silently. There were certainly opportunities for newspapers to seek active engagement with their readers before the advent of the social web, yet few did so consistently. The Pulitzer Center treats its journalists' work as ongoing conversations, convening public forums that welcome audience participation and seeking out other ways to draw in the public and spark discussions. Social and new media are an integral part of this outreach.

The Pulitzer Center has a main Twitter account @Pulitzercenter, which at this writing has some 18,000 followers who receive five to ten updates per day that engage community members with the reporting, asking and answering questions related to the center's reporting projects, and the issues that surface from the communication of the news and projects. The education community can engage through @PulitzerGateway, an account that highlights the center's education work with middle and secondary schools.

Similarly, the center's Facebook and Tumblr accounts are active—sharing reports, prompting conversations, and providing windows into Pulitzer Center work that match the voices of the communities that those services have come to foster. A testament to the rewards that such experimentation can bring has been the runaway success of the center's *In the Field* Tumblr, an account created to showcase journalism in progress. The conversational, behind-the-scenes tone of *In the Field* attracted some 15,000 Tumblr followers in just three weeks after the site was launched.

These social platforms present ways for the Pulitzer Center to find participatory audiences for its reporting while the reporting projects are underway, at the time they are published and long after publication. Most of the issues that are covered, after all, are evergreen. Next month there will be little to say about today's celebrity flameout or an NFL controversy, but global warming, food shortages, and population pressures will be with us for the foreseeable future, and the reporting projects that address them will continue to have relevance and resonance and will indeed build on each other, creating a mutually reinforcing body of work that presents the issues with breadth and depth.

Bringing Digital and Global Literacy to the Classroom

Not only does the Pulitzer Center sponsor interactive journalism projects and outreach activities for schools, but it also provides printed, audio, video, and digital resources that teachers and students alike can use in a variety of ways. For example, with the beginning of Paul Salopek's walk, the Pulitzer Center has commissioned a curriculum unit that teachers of all levels and subjects can use to create an introduction to the walk. The units are available for elementary, middle school, and high school students with the same basic theme for each level. These units focus on students getting to know who they are today as a result of their ancestors' movements across the globe from the beginning of mankind. The units are aligned to the Common Core State Standards and contain the following components: Big Ideas and Enduring Understandings, Essential Questions, Content, Skills and Strategies, Key Terms and Vocabulary, Learning Plan and Activities, Assessments, and Resources. All of the components are aligned to each other and the Common Core State Standards.

The Learning Plan and Activities section includes digital tools for students to use in completing the activities, which provide practice in mastering the content, using the skills, and employing the digital tools. The Resources section provides additional information and tools for the teachers and students during the unit. These units are based on the work of Heidi Hayes Jacobs in curriculum mapping and Jay McTighe and Grant Wiggins's work in backwards design. This unit design focuses on aligning all aspects of the learning for students. When the assessments are aligned to all of the other components of the unit, the data obtained from the assessments can better inform the teacher's instruction. Also, the addition of the use of digital tools in the activities that students perform as practice for the assessments allows the students to use technologies that they already use each day in their lives outside of school.

For years, the media landscape has been changing and has been engaging students, their families, and the general public in an unprecedented flow of information and sharing of news, conversations, debates, and ideas. People now have access to almost any information that they desire and are inundated with instant messages, email, and videos. But a question remains: Have all parts of our society kept up with the almost instant flow of information? The answer to this question is a resounding *no*. Educators have struggled to integrate the changing technology and media into the learning process. Many public schools ban the use of cell phones and other digital tools to keep distractions at a minimum, while other schools have embraced the technology of cell phones, tablets, and other digital devices as tools for learning. Unfortunately, the proliferation of these new tools for learning is creating a gap between the students and schools that can afford to purchase them and those who cannot. In addition, another gap exists between teachers and parents, who are slow to give up the traditional ways of gaining information they have used for years, and their students and children who are immersed in communicating, researching, and learning with technology.

Literacy for many teachers and parents consists of reading printed materials and obtaining news and other information from television or the computer. Lingering over the morning newspaper is a ritual that many people are not willing to abandon, even when they read the "paper" on their computers. In addition, people may have moved from reading books in print to reading those same texts on a digital reader, but education is moving much more slowly than the development of digital devices that can be used to obtain, share, and discuss and debate information.

Schools have been struggling with finding an appropriate use in their classrooms for the technologies that students use at home. Students, however, use technology and social media routinely each day to communicate with others in their lives, keep abreast of what is happening in the world, solve problems that arise, and be creative. In a school or classroom that does not employ any use of technology, students are not as easily engaged in learning and communication. They are outside of their comfort zones. For this reason, some of the activities listed in the Learning Plan and Activities section of the curriculum units on the Pulitzer Center site suggest interaction with other people around the globe and list tools classrooms can use to connect with each other and share their learning on a global issue, such as international adoption or a global learning activity like Salopek's walk around the globe. These various units utilizing the Gateways on the Pulitzer Center site and the units for the Out of Eden introduction enlist the use of technology in the activities that students complete to engage them in the practice, to make them feel comfortable in learning with tools that they use every day, and to increase their media and global literacy. These units are listed on the Pulitzer Center website along with the elementary, middle school, and high school units for Salopek's walk (http://pulitzercenter.org/node/11012/education).

At Washington International School, an independent K–12 international school of some one thousand students located in Washington, DC, the middle school teachers have embraced the Salopek project as an opportunity to connect the students' work on mapping and migration to current events in a multimedia context. During Salopek's visit to the school in November 2012, the sixth grade, for example, created detailed map routes for the first year of Salopek's walk. After a morning presentation when he described broadly the goals and methods of the walk, the sixth-grade students broke into groups of five and were tasked with researching possible routes he might take from Addis Ababa, the walk's approximate starting line, to Amman, Jordan, roughly its one-year endpoint. The students debated the relative pros and cons of taking an African route through western Sudan and Egypt versus an Arabian route, which would require a short boat ride to the southwest coast of Yemen, followed by a walk up through Saudi Arabia. They researched these routes as teams over two class periods using Internet resources and consulting with Salopek himself occasionally. Politics, climate, populations, culture, and terrain all factored into their recommendations; some groups presented as many as five different routes, providing detailed explanations of the relative merits of each.

As Salopek progressed during the spring of 2013, the students followed along and compared their recommendations and expectations to his reality through live Skype chats and other online interactions. In the late spring, their teachers set aside a multiday period when the students worked together to create a usable map by contributing their own research to one Google Map, using Salopek's findings and their own investigations to label the map with markers, photographs, and other data to show how the regions along the route would look, feel, and interact with a person walking on foot.

Conclusion

In journalism and education, this is certainly a time of upheaval. Journalistic models are changing from a single type of media usage to a collage of media types being used to create news and information that has the ability to engage as well as create empathy among consumers. Models like those created by the Pulitzer Center will spark discussions and debate on subjects of global interest long after what is considered a traditional news cycle, because journalists will be using a blend of new and old methods to reach out to consumers whose questions and suggestions will compose a rich variety of avenues to approach and follow up on global subjects.

Modern web-based storytelling can reach learners in a variety of ways. The Pulitzer Center's *Voices From Haiti* website uses technology to weave striking visual images, poetry in both English and Jamaican Creole, and long-form journalism into a multimedia platform that invites students into the lives of people whom they may have never considered before.

The social web allows students to become active participants in the news. No longer does the story end with the concluding paragraph of a newspaper article. When a particular news piece is treated as part of an ongoing communications campaign around a unifying global challenge like food security or climate change, new technologies can play a vital role. Students can have a conversation on Twitter using the hashtag #WhoMadeMy to explore the origins of the goods they buy every day. They can pull back the curtain on the process of professional reporting by following *In the Field* on Tumblr. And they can connect with journalists and subjects using these platforms whether they live in Skokie, Stockholm, or São Paolo.

The wide proliferation of information that has come with the explosion of the Internet since the mid-1990s has empowered students to become self-directed learners. A limitless pool of knowledge waits for anyone with access to a computer, an Internet connection, and a curious mind. But with the decline of the old gatekeepers of information—encyclopedia editors, textbook authors, and, of course, journalists—comes a responsibility for learners at ever-younger ages to become digitally literate consumers. They must be able to recognize bias and misinformation, hate speech disguised as facts, and other distortions.

But true digital literacy means more than simply recognizing lies on the Internet. Young people who subsist on a diet of Facebook updates, BuzzFeed lists, and cat gifs today will not become the effective global citizens we will need to tackle the systemic problems that await. They will need to nurture a healthy media diet through the development of good news-consumption habits.

By supporting quality, mixed-media global journalism projects, making the work freely available on its website, and driving conversations around the issues through broad public outreach and social media, the Pulitzer Center seeks to maintain the best principles of old journalism while making use of new technological tools to find and nurture new audiences.

Its education program leverages the reporting projects and the talents of the journalists who created them to encourage students to pursue similar explorations in their communities. Video and photography programs and writing contests promote creativity, empathy, media literacy, and technological competence. Often they result in student work that is relevant on a local and global scale. Even if students do not plan to become reporters themselves, the skillset of a modern journalist with a global beat is one that will serve young people well in the workplace they will soon enter.

References and Resources

Badkhen, A. (2011, September 12). *Reporting: Escaping the heat—Ice cream in Afghanistan* [Video file]. Accessed at http://pulitzercenter.org/reporting/afghanistan-heat-index-temperatures-taliban-poverty-violence on December 10, 2012.

Dawes, K. (n.d.). *Mothers of mothers* [Video file]. Accessed at http://pulitzercenter.org/features/voices-haiti on December 10, 2012.

Free Spirit Media. (2010, August 13). *It's their life: LGBT youth in Chicago* [Video file]. Accessed at www.freespiritmedia.org/work/video/Its-Their-Life-LGBT-Youth-in-Chicago on December 10, 2012.

Jacobs, H. H. (Ed.). (2004). *Getting results with curriculum mapping.* Alexandria, VA: Association for Supervision and Curriculum Development.

McTighe, J., & Wiggins, G. (1998). *Understanding by design.* Alexandria, VA: Association for Supervision and Curriculum Development.

Moeller, B., & Reitzes, T. (2011). *Integrating technology with student-centered learning: A report to the Nellie Mae Education Foundation.* Accessed at www.nmefoundation.org/resources/personalization/integrating-technology-with-student-centered-learning on August 29, 2013.

National Geographic & Knight Foundation. (n.d.). *Out of Eden walk: A journey through time.* Accessed at http://outofedenwalk.com on December 10, 2012.

Out of Eden: Knight Foundation site. (n.d.). *Out of Eden walk: A journey through time.* Accessed at www.outofedenwalk.com on December 10, 2012.

Out of Eden: National Geographic site. (n.d.) *Out of Eden walk: A journey through time.* Accessed at http://outofedenwalk.nationalgeographic.com on December 10, 2012.

Project Zero. (n.d.) *Walk to learn: A window into Project Zero's learning community for the Out of Eden walk.* Accessed at http://walktolearn.outofedenwalk.com on December 10, 2012.

Pulitzer Center on Crisis Reporting. (n.d.a). *Gateways.* Accessed at http://pulitzer center.org/gateways on December 10, 2012.

Pulitzer Center on Crisis Reporting. (n.d.b). *Voices from Haiti.* Accessed at http:// pulitzercenter.org/features/voices-haiti on December 10, 2012.

Pulitzer Center on Crisis Reporting. (n.d.c) *Women, children, crisis.* Accessed at http://pulitzercenter.org/women-children-crisis on December 10, 2012.

Tumblr. (n.d.). *Pulitzer Center field notes.* Accessed at http://pulitzerfieldnotes .tumblr.com on December 10, 2012.

Shirky, C. (2009, March 13). *Newspapers and thinking the unthinkable* [Web log post]. Accessed at www.shirky.com/weblog/2009/03/newspapers-and-thinking-the -unthinkable on December 10, 2012.

Index

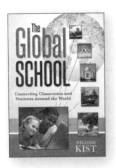

The Global School
William Kist
Prepare students for an increasingly flat world where diverse people from divergent cultures learn and work together rather than in isolation. Learn specific steps to globalize your classroom and encourage higher-order thinking, all wrapped in a 21st century skills framework.
BKF570

21st Century Skills
Edited by James A. Bellanca and Ron Brandt
Examine the Framework for 21st Century Learning from the Partnership for 21st Century Skills as a way to re-envision learning in a rapidly evolving global and technological world. Learn why these skills are necessary, which are most important, and how to best help schools include them.
BKF389

Bringing Innovation to School
Suzie Boss
Activate your students' creativity and problem-solving potential with breakthrough learning projects. Across all grades and content areas, student-driven, collaborative projects will teach students how to generate innovative ideas and then put them into action.
BKF546

Creating a Digital-Rich Classroom
Meg Ormiston
Design and deliver standards-based lessons in which technology plays an integral role. This book provides a research base and practical strategies for using web 2.0 tools to create engaging lessons that transform and enrich content.
BKF385

Solution Tree | Press
a division of
Solution Tree

Visit solution-tree.com or call 800.733.6786 to order.

Wait! Your professional development journey doesn't have to end with the last pages of this book.

We realize improving student learning doesn't happen overnight. And your school or district shouldn't be left to puzzle out all the details of this process alone.

No matter where you are on the journey, we're committed to helping you get to the next stage.

Take advantage of everything from **custom workshops** to **keynote presentations** and **interactive web and video conferencing**. We can even help you develop an action plan tailored to fit your specific needs.

Let's get the conversation started.

Call 888.763.9045 today.